my
KITCHEN
TABLE

100 Meals in Minutes

KITCHEN TABLE gives you a wealth of recipes from your favourite chefs. Whether you want a quick weekday supper, sumptuous weekend feast or food for friends and family, let Rick, Ken, Madhur, Antonio, Ainsley, Mary and Annabel bring their expertise to your table.

For exclusive recipes, our regular newsletter, blog and news about Apps for your phone, visit www.mykitchentable.co.uk

Throughout this book, when you see visit our site for practical videos, tips and hints from the My Kitchen Table team.

KITCHEN
TABLE

100 Meals in Minutes

AINSLEY
HARRIOTT

www.mykitchentable.co.uk

Welcome to *my* KITCHEN TABLE

I've gathered here **100 of my favourite meals in minutes** – each one simple to cook and packed with sensational flavours. Each dish can be cooked in less than an hour, so they're perfect for busy people who love delicious food.

Contents

Pomegranate, Orange and Mint Salad

This salad makes a refreshing starter on a hot day, and is also good as a side salad or between courses as a palate cleanser. For a more substantial meal, feta cheese would be a great addition. So simple, yet delicious …

Step one To get lovely slices of orange without any bitter pith, use a small sharp knife to take a slice off the top and bottom of the oranges so you can see the juicy flesh, then place on a chopping board. Carefully cut away the skin and pith, following the curve of the orange. Cut the fruit into horizontal slices, reserving any juice for the dressing.

Step two Arrange the orange slices on a large glass serving dish and sprinkle over the pomegranate seeds.

Step three To make the dressing whisk together the olive oil, orange juice and any reserved pomegranate juice in a small bowl. Season to taste and drizzle over the salad. Scatter the mint leaves over the salad and serve.

Here's a quick tip for removing pomegranate seeds: cut the fruit in half, use a spoon to scrape out some of the seeds, then turn the fruit inside-out and scrape again.

Serves 4

5–6 large oranges, plus 6 tbsp freshly squeezed orange juice

1 large pomegranate, seeds removed and any juices reserved (see tip)

2 tbsp olive oil

1 tbsp fresh mint leaves

salt and freshly ground black pepper

For a video masterclass on knife skills, go to
www.mykitchentable.co.uk/videos/knifeskills

Crispy Parma Ham and Asparagus Salad

This is a gorgeous salad that could be served as a starter or as a main meal. When in season, try to use home-grown asparagus. A glass or two of chilled white wine is the perfect accompaniment to this dish.

Serves 4

6 eggs

250g (9oz) asparagus

25g (1oz) butter

a squeeze of fresh lemon juice

8 slices Parma ham, about 85g (3¼ oz) in total

salt and freshly ground black pepper

to serve

Parmesan shavings

Step one Cook the eggs in a pan of boiling water for exactly 8 minutes. Meanwhile, sit a steamer or colander over the eggs, put in the asparagus, cover and cook for 4–5 minutes until just tender – alternatively, cook them in a pan of boiling water for 2–3 minutes. Meanwhile, preheat a ridged griddle pan or heavy, non-stick frying pan.

Step two Drain the eggs and asparagus and cool under cold water. Melt the butter in a small pan then, with a wire whisk, beat in some lemon juice and salt and pepper to taste.

Step three Cook the slices of Parma ham in the hot griddle pan, two at a time, for 30 seconds on each side. Set aside on kitchen paper. Cook the asparagus in the pan (making good use of the fat left from the Parma ham) for 2–3 minutes to give light bar-marks.

Step four Shell and halve the eggs and arrange on four plates along with the asparagus, topped with the crispy Parma ham. Drizzle over the lemon-butter dressing. Scatter over the shaved Parmesan and top with a good grind of black pepper.

Parma Fired Figs with Goats' Cheese Filling

Use fully ripe, fragrant figs for this recipe. It's a true melt-in-the-mouth experience that can be griddled or cooked outside on the barbie.

Step one Cut a deep cross in the top of each fig, cutting right down to, but not through, the base. Cut the goats' cheese into quarters. Open out the figs, slip a wedge of cheese into each, season with plenty of black pepper, then close the figs back together. Place a thyme sprig on the side of each fig and wrap the Parma ham round each one, enclosing the thyme sprigs.

Step two Griddle or cook over hot coals for 4–5 minutes, rolling the figs on their sides until the Parma ham is crispy and ruffled around the edges.

Step three Arrange small piles of rocket leaves in the centre of four serving plates and place a fig on top. Drizzle around a little olive oil and scatter over some rock salt and freshly ground black pepper.

Serves 4

4 ripe black figs

75g (3oz) soft goats' cheese

4 sprigs fresh thyme

4 slices Parma ham

freshly ground black pepper

to serve

rocket leaves

olive oil

rock salt

Hot-smoked Salmon with Avocado and Pink Grapefruit Salad

This tangy, refreshing salad uses hot-smoked salmon, which you can find in most good supermarkets and many delis. It's really delicious and quite different from the usual smoked salmon as you buy it as a whole fillet instead of thin slices.

Serves 4

2 pink or ruby grapefruit

1 small red onion

2 avocados

4 heads mixed red and white chicory

150g (5oz) hot-smoked salmon

50g (2oz) toasted pecan nuts, roughly chopped

for the dressing

1 tsp Dijon mustard

1 tbsp white wine vinegar

3 tbsp extra-virgin olive oil or avocado oil

salt and freshly ground black pepper

to serve

2 tbsp roughly chopped fresh flat-leaf parsley

Step one Peel the grapefruit by cutting a slice from the top of the fruit to expose the flesh, then remove the skin as you would peel an apple, cutting just beneath the white pith. Hold the peeled fruit in the palm of your hand and carefully cut out each segment between the thin lines of pith – do this over a bowl so that you can catch all the juices.

Step two Cut the onion in half and slice as finely as possible. Cut the avocados in half lengthways, discard the stones and skin, then slice or cube the flesh. Add to the grapefruit, along with the onion.

Step three To make the dressing, whisk together the mustard, vinegar and oil in a small bowl and season well.

Step four Trim the stalks from the chicory, separate the leaves and arrange on four plates. Put the grapefruit mixture on top, then flake the salmon and scatter it over the salads. Drizzle with the dressing, scatter over the pecans and parsley, and serve.

The sharp but not too sour flavour of the grapefruit marries well with all types of smoked fish: you could also use smoked mackerel or trout in this recipe. Choose a grapefruit that is heavy for its size – a sign of juiciness – and that has a good, plump skin.

Filo Baskets with Black and Blue

Black pudding and melted blue cheese is a really tasty combination. Look out for the authentic Greek filo pastry, it really is a superior product; once you've opened the packet, cover the pastry with a damp cloth until ready to use to prevent it from drying out.

Step one Preheat the oven to 180°C/350°F/gas 4. Melt the butter in a small pan or in the microwave and leave to cool. Unfold the filo pastry and cut the sheets into quarters, then cover with a damp tea towel.

Step two Take 4 x 200ml (7fl oz) glass ramekins and place them upside down on a non-stick baking sheet. Take a piece of filo, brush with butter, then place buttered-side down over the base of the ramekin. Add two more layers of buttered filo pastry, placing each square at a slightly different angle. Repeat the process for all the ramekins.

Step three Bake the filo baskets for 10–12 minutes until just cooked through and lightly golden. Remove from the oven but do not turn the oven off. When the filo baskets are cool enough to handle, carefully lift them from the ramekins, then transfer to a wire rack and leave to cool completely.

Step four Heat the sunflower oil in a heavy-based frying pan and sauté the black pudding for a minute or so on each side until lightly crisp.

Step five Drop a heaped tablespoon of the onion marmalade into each filo basket and arrange two slices of black pudding on top. Scatter over the Cashel Blue and set on a baking sheet. Bake for a further 5–6 minutes, until the Cashel Blue is melted and bubbling. Arrange on plates and garnish each basket with a teaspoon of the onion marmalade to serve.

This recipe would also work well as bite-sized canapés, using mini muffin trays to make the baskets.

Serves 4

50g (2oz) unsalted butter

3 sheets filo pastry, thawed if frozen

1 tsp sunflower oil

200g (7oz) black pudding, casing removed and cut into 8 slices

6 heaped tbsp onion marmalade (from a jar), plus extra to serve

100g (4oz) Cashel Blue cheese, crumbled

Mushroom, Almond and Garlic Soup

I like this soup lovely and thick, but if you prefer it thinner feel free to add more stock or a good splash of water. It is best to do this after you have blitzed the soup and added the cream, as the consistency will alter at this stage. Ring the changes when making this soup by varying the type of mushrooms you use – chestnut taste good, or you could try mixing two different varieties.

Serves 4

2 tbsp olive oil, plus extra for drizzling

25g (1oz) unsalted butter

1 onion, halved and thinly sliced

3 garlic cloves, crushed

250g (9oz) button mushrooms, sliced

150ml (¼ pint) white wine

300ml (½ pint) vegetable stock

50g (2oz) ground almonds

50g (2oz) flaked almonds, toasted

120ml (4fl oz) double cream

salt and freshly ground black pepper

to serve

a few sprigs of fresh flat-leaf parsley

chunks of granary bread (optional)

Step one Heat the oil and butter in a large, heavy-based pan. Tip in the onion and garlic and fry gently over a medium heat for 3 minutes until softened but not browned, stirring occasionally. Add the mushrooms and cook for a further 2 minutes, stirring. Pour in the wine, increase the heat and allow the wine to bubble and reduce for 1 minute.

Step two Add the stock, ground almonds and half the flaked almonds, reserving the remainder to use as a garnish. Bring to the boil, then reduce the heat and simmer, uncovered, for 5 minutes, stirring occasionally.

Step three Transfer the soup into a food-processor and blend to a purée (or use a hand blender), then gradually pour in the cream. Pour the soup back into the pan, season to taste and reheat gently. Ladle the soup into warmed serving bowls and scatter over the reserved almonds. Drizzle over a teaspoon of olive oil and add a parsley sprig to each bowl. Serve with chunks of granary bread on the side, if liked.

Red Lentil Soup with Lemon Yoghurt

This delicious and substantial vegetarian soup is a perfect warming dish for a cold winter's night. The red lentils are used to make a thick and tasty base to this soup. Alternatively, you could use yellow split peas, but these need soaking overnight before cooking.

Step one Heat the oil in a large pan and cook the onion, carrots and thyme for about 3–4 minutes until beginning to soften. Add the garlic, chilli and mustard seeds and cook for a further couple of minutes.

Step two Stir in the tomatoes, lentils and stock. Bring to the boil. Reduce the heat, cover and simmer gently for 30 minutes until the lentils are tender and easy to crush.

Step three Mix together the yoghurt, half the lemon zest and season to taste. Drizzle the lemon juice into the soup and season with salt and pepper. Ladle the soup into warmed serving bowls, top with a spoonful of the lemon yoghurt and scatter over the remaining lemon zest and some freshly ground black pepper.

To prepare ahead you can make the soup up to the end of the lentil cooking time, then cool it thoroughly and freeze for up to a month. Defrost before reheating and completing the soup.

Serves 4

1 tbsp olive oil

1 onion, finely chopped

2 carrots, finely diced

leaves from 1 sprig of fresh thyme

2 garlic cloves, finely chopped

1 red chilli, seeded and finely diced

1 tsp yellow mustard seeds

3 tomatoes, roughly diced

100g (4oz) dried red lentils

1.2 litres (2 pints) vegetable stock

4 tbsp Greek yoghurt

finely grated zest and juice of 1 small lemon

salt and freshly ground black pepper

Have you made this recipe? Tell us what you think at
www.mykitchentable.co.uk/blog

19

Thai Lemon Grass, Chicken and Mushroom Broth

I've used chicken for this recipe but you could also use diced prawns or minced pork. For a lovely winter warmer that will keep the chill at bay, stir in a handful of shredded ginger.

Serves 2

1 lemon grass stalk

600ml (1 pint) hot chicken stock

2 skinless, boneless chicken breasts, diced

1–2 tsp Thai red curry paste (see tip)

1 shallot, finely chopped

100g (4oz) shiitake mushrooms, sliced, or tinned straw mushrooms, halved

2 tsp light muscovado sugar

1 tsp Thai fish sauce

juice of 1 lemon

1 spring onion, thinly sliced

1 red chilli, seeded and thinly sliced

2 tbsp fresh coriander leaves

salt and freshly ground black pepper

to serve

lemon wedges (optional)

Step one Flatten the lemon grass stalk with a rolling pin or meat mallet. Put in a large pan and add the stock, chicken, curry paste and shallot, and bring to the boil. Add the mushrooms, reduce the heat and simmer gently for 8–10 minutes.

Step two Stir the sugar and fish sauce and leave to simmer for a further 3 minutes until the chicken is cooked. Squeeze in the lemon juice and season to taste. Ladle the soup into warmed serving bowls and scatter over the onion, chilli and coriander. Serve with an extra wedge of lemon, if liked.

Here's my own low-fat version of Thai red curry paste: into a food-processor, put 1 small roughly chopped red onion, 4 garlic cloves, a 5cm (2in) piece of fresh root ginger or galangal (peeled and roughly chopped), 6 red Thai chillies (remove the seeds for a milder flavour) and 1 lemon grass stalk (tough outer leaves removed and inner stalk roughly chopped). Process to a coarse paste. Add ½ teaspoon salt, 1 teaspoon coriander seeds and the juice and finely grated rind of 1 lime, and purée until smooth. Keep in an airtight jar in the fridge for up to 2 weeks.

Pea, Mint and Spinach Soup

This beautiful bright-green soup is a taste of spring, but it can be enjoyed at any time of the year. Use frozen peas rather than fresh ones as they give a much better texture. This recipe creates very little washing-up – just blend the soup base until smooth, add the peas and spinach and blend again.

Step one Heat the oil and butter in a large saucepan. Add the onion and leek and cook over a low heat for about 10 minutes, until tender but not coloured. Add the garlic and cook for a further 30 seconds.

Step two Add the potatoes to the pan, pour in the stock and bring to the boil. Reduce the heat and simmer over a gentle heat for 15 minutes or until the potatoes are tender when tested with the point of a knife.

Step three Pour the soup into a blender and whizz until smooth. Add the peas and spinach and blend again until the soup is bright green and almost smooth. Pour back into the pan, add the mint, then season and reheat gently. Pour the soup into warmed serving bowls, add a dollop of crème fraîche and a twist of pepper, and serve.

Serves 4–6

1 tbsp olive oil

25g (1oz) butter

1 onion, chopped

1 leek, chopped

1 fat garlic clove, crushed

225g (8oz) floury potatoes such as Maris Piper or King Edward, chopped

1.2 litres (2 pints) vegetable stock

250g (9oz) frozen garden peas, defrosted

75g (3oz) young leaf spinach

2 tbsp chopped fresh mint

salt and freshly ground black pepper

to serve

crème fraîche

Chorizo Chowder

This warming soup, makes a really satisfying winter supper or weekend lunch. Make sure you buy whole chorizo sausages and slice them yourself, as the slices in packets of pre-cut chorizo are too thin for this soup.

Serves 4

a knob of butter

1 small onion, finely chopped

4 garlic cloves, chopped

500g (1lb 2oz) floury potatoes such as Maris Piper or King Edward, cubed

1 leek, thinly sliced

1 tsp cayenne pepper

1 litre (1¾ pints) vegetable stock

250g (9oz) chorizo sausage, cut into 1cm (½ in) wide slices, or 1cm (½ in) dice

salt and freshly ground black pepper

to serve

sprigs of flat-leaf parsley

crusty bread (optional)

Step one Heat the butter in a large pan and cook the onion, garlic and potatoes for 5 minutes until lightly golden. Add the leek and cayenne pepper and cook for a further 1 minute.

Step two Add the stock and bring to the boil, then reduce the heat and simmer for 20 minutes until the potatoes are very soft and beginning to break up into the soup.

Step three Using a potato masher, roughly mash the potatoes into the soup. Stir in the chorizo and simmer gently for 5 minutes until the orange-coloured oil from the chorizo rises to the surface of the soup. Season to taste, ladle into serving bowls and garnish with sprigs of flat-leaf parsley. Serve with lots of crusty bread for mopping up.

Prawn and Coconut Laksa

In Thailand they refer to this dish as *sanuk*, which means 'enjoyable and good fun', or *sabai*, meaning 'deliciously satisfied'.

Step one To make the curry paste, place all the ingredients for the paste in a food-processor or blender. Add 75ml (2¾fl oz) of the coconut milk and whizz to a paste, scraping down the sides with a rubber spatula.

Step two Heat the oil in a large pan, add the curry paste and cook for 2 minutes over a lowish heat to allow all the ingredients to release their delicious aromas. Add the remaining coconut milk, stock, fish sauce and brown sugar. Bring to the boil, reduce the heat and simmer very gently for 10–15 minutes. Meanwhile, cook the noodles in boiling water according to the packet instructions.

Step three Add the prawns to the broth and simmer until they change colour and are cooked through. Add the beansprouts and cook for a further 30 seconds. Divide the noodles between four warmed bowls and ladle the soup, prawns and beansprouts on top. Scatter with the spring onions and coriander, and serve with lime wedges to squeeze over.

The paste for this dish can be made in advance and kept in the fridge or freezer. The coconut broth is a base to which all sorts of foods can be added: try it with fresh fish or cooked chicken, rice noodles, bamboo shoots or pak choy leaves.

Serves 4

1 x 400ml (14fl oz) tin coconut milk

2 tbsp sunflower oil

400ml (14fl oz) light chicken or fish stock

1 tbsp fish sauce

1 tbsp soft light brown sugar

250g (9oz) fine egg noodles

24 raw tiger prawns, shelled and deveined

100g (4oz) beansprouts, rinsed

4 spring onions, chopped

2 tbsp coriander, roughly chopped

4 lime wedges

for the curry paste

1 red chilli, seeded and chopped

1 stick lemon grass, roughly chopped

1 tbsp ginger, freshly grated

1 tsp ground turmeric

1 tsp ground coriander

2 garlic cloves, crushed

2 shallots, roughly chopped

Roquefort, Apple and Walnut Salad

Toasting the walnuts in this recipe brings out the natural oils, makes them crisper and intensifies the flavour. Any crumbly cheese – Stilton, Cheshire, Lancashire or feta – can go with this salad, but for me the semi-soft Roquefort wins every time. Walnut oil can be used in place of extra-virgin olive oil.

Serves 4

2 Braeburn apples

juice of ½ lemon

6 spring onions, trimmed

150g (5oz) raw beetroot

150g (5oz) mixed watercress and wild rocket

75g (3oz) toasted walnuts

100g (4oz) Roquefort cheese, crumbled

25g (1oz) pecorino shavings

for the dressing

1 tsp wholegrain mustard

1 tbsp white wine or cider vinegar

4 tbsp extra-virgin olive oil

1 tsp clear honey

salt and freshly ground black pepper

to serve

chunks of crusty bread

Step one Quarter, core and slice the apples. Toss in the lemon juice to prevent them discolouring. Thinly slice the spring onions diagonally. Peel the beetroot, then cut it into fine matchsticks or grate coarsely.

Step two Put all the dressing ingredients in a small bowl, add seasoning and whisk until combined.

Step three Place a handful of watercress and rocket in four bowls and arrange the apples, spring onions and beetroot on top. Scatter over the walnuts and Roquefort. Drizzle with the dressing, top with the pecorino and serve with crusty bread.

When preparing the beetroot, wear gloves to prevent it staining your hands, or use clingfilm to hold it.

Maryland Crabcakes with Caper Salsa

Maryland crabcakes are traditionally coated in breadcrumbs or cornmeal, but this recipe is much simpler. Before you make the patties, have a taste of the mixture and add a splash more Tabasco or Worcestershire sauce if you think it needs it.

Step one Preheat the oven to 100°C/200°F/gas ⅓. In a large bowl, combine the crabmeat, egg, salad onions, mayonnaise, mustard, herbs, Worcestershire sauce, Tabasco and the crushed crackers, mixing the ingredients together with a fork. Season to taste. Divide the mixture into 12 portions. Using slightly wet hands, form into balls and then flatten slightly into small patties; set aside.

Step two To make the salsa, place the capers in a small bowl with the tomatoes, dill and half the oil. Cut the lemon in half, finely grate the zest from one half into the salsa, then from the same half squeeze in the juice and mix. Season to taste. Cut the remaining lemon half into 4 wedges and set aside to use later as a garnish.

Step three Heat 1 tablespoon of oil in a large non-stick frying pan. Add half the crabcakes and cook for 3 minutes on each side until heated through and lightly golden. Remove from the pan, drain on kitchen paper and keep warm in the oven. Heat the remaining oil and cook the remaining crabcakes in the same way. Garnish with the dill sprigs and lemon wedges and serve with the salsa.

The crushed cream crackers add a lovely texture; the easiest way to crush them is to put them in a bag and bash them with a rolling pin, or you could blitz them briefly in a food-processor.

Serves 4

350g (12oz) fresh white crabmeat

1 egg, lightly beaten

2 spring onions, thinly sliced

2 tbsp mayonnaise

1 tsp Dijon mustard

2 tbsp chopped fresh flat-leaf parsley

1 tsp chopped fresh thyme (optional)

a dash of Worcestershire sauce

a good dash of Tabasco sauce

50g (2oz) cream crackers, crushed

for the caper salsa

100g (4oz) capers, drained and rinsed

2 ripe tomatoes, seeded and diced

1 tbsp chopped fresh dill, plus extra sprigs to garnish

4 tbsp olive oil

1 lemon

salt and freshly ground black pepper

Brie Quesadillas

These gorgeous treats are a perfect snack anytime – me and my mates love them at half time when we're watching the footie – and you can use all sorts of fillings. They can be prepared up to one hour in advance, covered with clingfilm and kept at room temperature; then simply reheat in the oven when you are ready to serve.

Serves 4–6

8 soft flour tortillas

olive oil, for brushing

350g (12oz) Brie, thinly sliced

1 mild red chilli, seeded and finely chopped

1 ripe mango, peeled, stoned and thinly sliced

2 spring onions, thinly sliced

salt and freshly ground black pepper

Step one Preheat the oven to 200°C/400°F/gas 6 and heat a ridged griddle pan over a medium heat until very hot. Brush one side of each tortilla with a little olive oil. Place one tortilla in the pan, oiled-side down, and cook for 1 minute until nicely marked, pressing down with a spatula. Repeat with the remaining tortillas.

Step two Set half the tortillas on baking sheets, marked-side down. Place a layer of Brie on each and then scatter over the chilli, mango and spring onions. Season to taste. Cover with the remaining tortillas, marked-side up, and bake for about 5 minutes or until heated through and the Brie has melted.

Step three Allow the quesadillas to cool slightly for ease of handling, then cut each one into eight wedges with a serrated knife, pizza cutter or kitchen scissors. To serve, arrange on warmed plates or one large platter.

Happy Cancun Chicken Chompers

These yummy little sticks always go down well at parties and they're great on the barbecue. The delicious chilli dipping sauce is the perfect accompaniment, so you might need to make extra. Happy chomping!

Step one Make the marinade first. Using a pestle and mortar, grind the peppercorns, garlic and coriander to make a paste. Mix in the sugar, lime juice, fish sauce, soy sauce and sunflower oil until well blended.

Step two Halve each chicken breast horizontally. Flatten each piece out with a rolling pin until 5mm (¼ in) thick. Cut each piece lengthways into strips 3cm (1¼ in) wide. Add to the marinade and set aside for up to 1 hour.

Step three Meanwhile, preheat the grill or light the barbecue, soak the wooden skewers and make the dipping sauce. Heat the vinegar and sugar together in a small pan, stirring until the sugar has dissolved. Bring to the boil then simmer for 3–4 minutes. Remove from the heat, stir in the chillies and salt and set aside to cool.

Step four Thread the chicken strips onto the skewers and cook over hot coals or under the grill for 4–5 minutes on each side until cooked through and well browned. Serve with rice noodles or plain boiled rice.

You can prepare the chicken 8 hours ahead. For convenience you might want to buy packets of mini chicken fillets instead of breast.

Serves 4

4 skinless, boneless chicken breasts, 75–100g (3–4oz) each

for the marinade

1 tsp black peppercorns

4 garlic cloves

2 tbsp fresh coriander leaves, plus extra to garnish

1 tsp caster sugar

juice of 1 lime

1 tsp Thai fish sauce

1 tsp light soy sauce

2 tsp sunflower oil

for the dipping sauce

75ml (3fl oz) red wine vinegar

75g (3oz) caster sugar

2 chillies, seeded and finely chopped

¼ tsp salt

to serve

rice noodles or plain boiled rice

For a video masterclass on using a pestle and mortar, go to
www.mykitchentable.co.uk/videos/pestlemortar

Apple Maple Pancakes with Blackberry Compote

It's such a shame that for many of us the only time we turn our hands to making pancakes is on Shrove Tuesday, because they are among the simplest and most satisfying things to make.

Makes 18–20

2 red-skinned eating apples

1 tbsp maple syrup

½ tsp ground cinnamon

2 tsp butter

150g (5oz) plain flour

½ tsp baking powder

pinch of salt

50g (2oz) caster sugar

175ml (6fl oz) milk

2 large eggs, separated

maple syrup, to serve

for the blackberry compote

300g (11oz) blackberries

1 tbsp caster sugar

Step one Make the compote first. Place the blackberries in a small pan, add the sugar and cook over a low heat until tender and juicy. Remove from the heat. Core but do not peel the apples, then slice into rings no thicker than a £1 coin. You will need at least 18–20 slices. Place them in a bowl, add the maple syrup and cinnamon and mix to coat.

Step two Melt half the butter in a large frying pan set over a medium heat. Add half the sliced apples and cook for 30–60 seconds, until starting to soften. Remove from the pan and cook the remaining apple slices. Wash and dry the frying pan.

Step three Sift the flour, baking powder and salt into a medium-sized bowl. Add the sugar and mix to combine. In a jug whisk together the milk and the egg yolks. Pour this into the dry ingredients and mix to make a smooth batter. In a clean bowl whisk the egg whites until they will just stand in stiff peaks. Gently fold into the batter.

Step four Lightly grease the pan with a little of the remaining butter and place over a medium heat. Arrange four apple slices in the pan, 4–5cm (1½–2in) apart and spoon 1 tablespoon of batter over each slice. Cook until small bubbles appear on the surface of the pancakes and their undersides are golden brown. Flip the pancakes over with a palette knife and cook for a further minute. Transfer to a plate and keep warm while you cook the remaining pancakes in the same way. You may need to wipe the pan clean with kitchen paper after each batch.

Step five Serve the warm pancakes with the blackberry compote spooned over and a generous glug of maple syrup.

Green Crunchy Vegetable Stir Fry with Cashews and Black Bean Sauce

This sounds healthy and tastes even better. The veggies I've listed are only a guideline, so feel free to use whatever is seasonal and available. You can't go wrong.

Step one Prepare all the vegetables before starting to cook. Slice the onion. If using the chilli, cut it in half lengthways, scrape out the seeds with a teaspoon and finely slice the flesh. Crush the garlic. Cut the courgettes in half lengthways, and cut each half diagonally into 1cm (½in) slices. Cut the asparagus into 2.5cm (1in) lengths. Finely slice the spring onions.

Step two Turn on the extractor fan and heat the oil in a wok. When hot, add the chilli (if using), garlic and three-quarters of the spring onions and stir fry over a medium to high heat for 2 minutes.

Step three Add the courgettes, asparagus, onion, sugarsnaps or mangetout and broccoli. Continue to stir fry for 4–5 minutes, until tender. Mix in the black bean sauce, evenly coating all the vegetables, and stir fry for a further 30–60 seconds. Scatter with the coriander, the remaining spring onions and the cashews, and serve with egg noodles or steamed rice.

Serves 4

1 onion

1 red or green chilli (optional)

1 garlic clove

2 courgettes

250g (9oz) asparagus, trimmed

3 spring onions, trimmed

2 tbsp sunflower or groundnut oil

100g (4oz) sugarsnaps or mangetout, trimmed

225g (8oz) small broccoli florets

3–4 tbsp black bean sauce

1 tbsp chopped fresh coriander

50g (2oz) toasted unsalted cashew nuts

to serve

egg noodles or steamed rice

For a video masterclass on chopping vegetables, go to
www.mykitchentable.co.uk/videos/choppingvegetables

Chickpea and Chorizo Fritters

These fritters are always a winner and make the perfect snack when your mates pop round for the footie. The main ingredient is gram (chickpea) flour, which is available from supermarkets, but you'll also find it in health-food shops.

Serves 4–6

¼ tsp cumin seeds

600ml (1 pint) milk

25g (1oz) unsalted butter

1 red chilli, seeded and finely chopped

1 garlic clove, crushed

150g (5oz) gram (chickpea) flour, sifted

2 tbsp olive oil

1 chorizo sausage (about 100g/4oz), finely diced

1 tbsp chopped fresh flat-leaf parsley

sunflower oil, for deep-frying

about 50g (2oz) polenta or semolina

salt and freshly ground black pepper

to serve

soured cream and chive dip

Step one Heat a small frying pan over a medium heat. Add the cumin seeds and toss and toast for 1 minute until aromatic. Place in a non-stick pan, add the milk, butter, chilli and garlic, and bring to the boil. Reduce the heat and slowly add the gram flour, stirring to combine. Cook gently for 5–6 minutes until thickened, beating occasionally with a wooden spatula.

Step two Meanwhile, heat the oil in a non-stick frying pan, tip in the chorizo and fry for a few minutes until sizzling and lightly golden. Pour into the gram flour mixture and the parsley, and mix until well combined. Season to taste.

Step three Line a 1.2 litre (2 pint) roasting tin or ovenproof dish with greaseproof paper and pour in the fritter mixture, using a plastic spatula. Level the top with the back of a spoon, cover with clingfilm and chill in the freezer for about 20 minutes or until cooled and set (or overnight in the fridge is best, if time allows). Meanwhile, preheat a deep fryer or fill a flat-bottomed wok one-third full with sunflower oil and heat to 190°C/375°F. (If you don't have a thermometer, the oil should be hot enough that when a cube of bread is added to the pan, it browns in about 40 seconds.)

Step four Turn the fritter mixture onto a work surface and peel away the paper. Cut into 7.5cm (3in) squares, then cut in half again, into triangles. Roll in the polenta or semolina to coat. Deep-fry the fritters in batches for 2–3 minutes until golden. Drain on kitchen paper and serve warm with the soured cream and chive dip.

Fennel, Pear and Parma Ham Salad

Whether sliced thinly and eaten raw, baked in a little stock for half an hour, or gently poached in sugar syrup and glazed, fennel is always delicious. This crunchy salad really captures its bittersweet taste, and ripe, flavoursome pear is a great contrast: I recommend the red-skinned variety Red Bartlett.

Step one Make the dressing first. Combine all the ingredients in a small bowl, add seasoning and whisk to combine.

Step two Trim the fennel and slice it as thinly as possible, using a mandolin or the thin setting on your food-processor (yes, the one you never use); otherwise it's a sharp knife by hand. Quarter and core the pears, slice thinly and toss in the lemon juice to prevent them discolouring. Slice the onion as thinly as you can. Add it, with the pears, to the fennel, crumble in the dolcelatte and toss lightly with your hands.

Step three Arrange the radicchio, rocket and endive on four plates. Pile the fennel salad on top, then tear the Parma ham into pieces and drape them over the salad. Scatter over the hazelnuts and drizzle with the dressing. Top with the Parmesan shavings if using and serve.

Bresaola can be used instead of Parma ham for this dish. If you like, you could keep the aniseedy fronds (dill weed) from the top of the fennel, and chop them up later and add to the salad.

Serves 4

1 large head fennel

2 ripe pears

juice of ½ lemon

1 red onion

150g (5oz) dolcelatte cheese

2 heads radicchio

handful of wild rocket

handful of curly endive

12 slices Parma ham or bresaola

100g (4oz) toasted hazelnuts, roughly chopped

salt and freshly ground black pepper

for the dressing

4 tbsp walnut or hazelnut oil

1 tbsp sherry vinegar

1 small shallot, finely diced

1 tsp clear honey

to serve

Parmesan shavings (optional)

Sweet Chilli Tomato Tarte Tatin

When making any tarte tatin recipe try to use a large, flat plate that is slightly larger than the ovenproof frying pan. This will enable you to turn out the tarte with much greater ease.

Serves 4

3 firm, ripe plum tomatoes

1 tbsp olive oil

1 small onion, chopped

2 garlic cloves, finely chopped

2 tbsp tomato purée

3 tbsp tomato passata

2 tbsp sweet chilli sauce

25 g (1 oz) unsalted butter

10 fresh basil leaves

225 g (8 oz) ready-rolled puff pastry, thawed if frozen

salt and freshly ground black pepper

to serve

lightly dressed green salad

Step one Preheat the oven to 220°C/425°F/gas 7. Slice the tomatoes, then arrange on kitchen paper to absorb some of the excess liquid. Heat a 23cm (9in) non-stick ovenproof frying pan or skillet. Pour in the olive oil and add the onion and garlic, then fry for about 3 minutes, stirring occasionally, until softened and just starting to brown.

Step two Add the tomato purée to the pan with the passata and chilli sauce, then cook over a moderate heat for about 3 minutes until you have achieved a reasonably thick paste. Remove from the heat, season with salt and pepper, then tip into a bowl and set aside.

Step three Wipe the pan clean and rub with the butter, making sure you go right up the sides. Arrange the tomato slices in a layer to cover the bottom of the pan and place the basil leaves in the gaps. Season to taste, then spread over the reserved tomato paste, being careful not to move the tomato slices or basil.

Step four Unroll the pastry and cut into a circle slightly larger than the frying pan, then carefully place over the layer of tomato paste. Tuck the pastry edges down the sides of the pan, like making a bed! Place in the oven and cook for 10 minutes, then reduce the oven temperature to 200°C/400°F/gas 6 and cook for another 15–20 minutes until the pastry is crisp and golden. Remove from the oven, allow to sit for 1 minute, then invert on to a plate (see introduction). If any tomatoes become loose, place them back into the tarte. Cut into wedges and serve with salad.

Pesto-rippled Scrambled Eggs

This is absolutely delicious, and the rippled effect comes not only from the pesto, but also from the egg yolks and whites being mixed together. But, be warned, it's worth sharing the finished dish with your partner as it contains raw garlic, which can have quite a long-lasting effect.

Step one Put the garlic and pine nuts in a mini food-processor and blitz until finely chopped. Add the basil and Parmesan and blitz again until well blended. Add the oil and some seasoning and pulse until well combined into a pesto.

Step two Heat the butter in a small pan and crack in the eggs, season, then leave to set for 2 minutes. With a wooden spoon, stir very gently so the eggs begin to set in clumps of white and yellow. Before the eggs have completely set, lightly stir in the pesto. Pile the scrambled eggs onto warm toast or bagels, scatter over the Parmesan and serve.

Serves 2

1 small garlic clove, roughly chopped

1 tbsp toasted pine nuts

15g fresh basil

1 tbsp freshly grated Parmesan, plus extra to serve

2–3 tbsp olive oil

large knob of butter

4 large eggs

salt and freshly ground black pepper

to serve

warm toasted bread or bagels, buttered

Spinach, Cheddar and Parmesan Muffins with a Cream Cheese Centre

We tend to think of muffins as sweet accompaniments to coffee, but savoury ones can be equally exciting, as you'll discover with these delightfully surprising cheesy muffins.

Makes 12

500g (1 lb 2oz) plain flour

4 tsp baking powder

pinch of salt

3 eggs, beaten

250ml (8fl oz) milk

50ml (2fl oz) olive oil, plus extra for greasing

100g (4oz) Cheddar, grated

75g (3oz) Parmesan, grated

150g (5oz) cooked spinach, finely chopped

1 tsp hot pepper sauce (optional)

200g (7oz) full-fat cream cheese

25g (1oz) sesame seeds

Step one Preheat the oven to 200°C/400°F/gas 6. Line a muffin tray with paper cases or grease the holes with a little oil. Sift the flour, baking powder and salt into a large bowl. Make a well in the centre of the flour, pour in the eggs, milk and oil and stir until just combined: do not overmix. Lightly fold in the two cheeses, spinach and hot pepper sauce if using.

Step two Half-fill the muffin holes or paper cases with the mixture, then pipe or spoon about a tablespoon of cream cheese on top of each and cover with the remaining mixture. Sprinkle the sesame seeds on the muffins and bake in the centre of the oven for 20–25 minutes, or until golden and cooked through. Remove the muffins from the tray while still warm and serve.

Huevos Rancheros

This is a Mexican dish of baked eggs on a sea of spiced peppers and tomatoes. There are many variations, including one from Tunisia, which is called *chakchouka* and has no chilli.

Step one Preheat the oven to 180°C/350°F/gas 4. Heat the oil in a 28cm (11in) ovenproof frying pan. Tip in the onion, garlic, peppers and chilli and fry over a medium heat for 4–5 minutes until softened but not coloured, stirring occasionally.

Step two Stir in the oregano, cumin, sugar and chopped tomatoes. Bring to a simmer, then cook for about 5 minutes until the peppers are completely tender and the sauce has slightly reduced and thickened. Season to taste.

Step three Using the back of a wooden spoon, make 4 holes in the pepper mixture just large enough to fit the eggs, then carefully crack an egg into each hole. Season to taste and bake for 10–12 minutes or until the egg whites are set but the yolks are still runny. Scatter over the chives to garnish and serve straight from the frying pan to the table, with plenty of crusty bread to mop up all the delicious juices.

Serves 4

1 tbsp olive oil

1 large onion, chopped

2 garlic cloves, crushed

1 red and 1 yellow pepper, halved, seeded and sliced

1 red chilli, seeded and finely diced

1 tsp dried oregano

½ tsp ground cumin

1 tbsp caster sugar

1 x 400g (14oz) tin chopped tomatoes

4 eggs

salt and freshly ground black pepper

to serve

fresh snipped chives

fresh crusty bread

Courgette, Coriander and Parmesan Röstis

Courgettes are such a versatile vegetable: here I've combined them with the freshness of lemon and the fragrance of coriander and accompanied them with a salad, and I'm sure these fritters will turn into a firm favourite.

Serves 4

550g (1¼ lb) courgettes, coarsely grated

100g (4oz) ground rice

3 tbsp shredded fresh coriander leaves

75g (3oz) Parmesan, freshly grated

1 egg, lightly beaten

1 tsp finely grated lemon zest, plus 1 tbsp lemon juice

50g (2oz) flaked almonds

120ml (4fl oz) olive oil

1 ripe tomato, seeded and finely diced

1 shallot, finely chopped

salt and freshly ground black pepper

to serve

100g (4oz) wild rocket or watercress

lemon wedges

Step one Preheat the oven to 100°C/200°F/gas ⅓. Squeeze the courgettes dry in a clean tea towel and tip into a large bowl. Mix in the ground rice, coriander, Parmesan, egg, lemon zest and almonds. Season to taste and divide into 16 evenly sized balls, then flatten slightly into patties.

Step two Heat 2 tablepoons of the olive oil in a large, non-stick frying pan. Carefully. add half the patties. Cook for 2–3 minutes on each side or until cooked through, crisp and golden. Drain on kitchen paper and keep warm in the oven. Repeat with a further 2 tablespoons of oil and the remaining patties.

Step three To make the dressing, place the remaining oil in a bowl and add the tomato, shallot and lemon juice, and season to taste. Whisk until well combined. Divide the salad leaves among serving plates and drizzle over the dressing. Add the fritters and garnish with the lemon wedges to serve.

Courgettes have a naturally high water content – squeezing them dry before they are fried ensures that the fritters are lovely and crisp when cooked.

Oozing Oriental Stuffed Aubergine Slices

It looks good, it tastes great and it's ideal for a special barbecue date, or just cook it under the grill. Get stuffing.

Step one Soak four 12cm (4½in) wooden skewers in water and light the barbecue or grill.

Step two Cut the aubergine diagonally into 16 oval slices, about 1cm (½in) thick. Brush each slice with oil on one side only, season and barbecue for 4–5 minutes over medium-hot coals, or cook under a medium grill, on one side only, until golden brown. Meanwhile, place the noodles in a bowl and cover with boiling water. Set aside for 2–3 minutes, or according to packet instructions, then drain.

Step three Mix together the carrot, ginger, coriander, sesame seeds, beansprouts, Hoisin sauce and soy sauce, and add the drained noodles. Place 8 slices of the aubergine, cooked side uppermost, on a flat surface and spoon noodle mixture into the centre of each. Top with the remaining aubergine slices, ensuring that the uncooked surface is on the outside.

Step four Using soaked 12cm (4½in) wooden skewers, pin each aubergine sandwich closed along the long edges, to enclose the filling. Brush with a little more oil and cook for 2–3 minutes on each side until the aubergine is cooked and golden. Serve drizzled with soy sauce on boiled rice.

Serves 4

2 large aubergines

sunflower oil, for brushing

50g (2oz) glass noodles, or other thin rice noodles

boiling water

1 large carrot, cut into matchsticks

2cm (¾in) piece fresh root ginger, finely chopped

a handful of fresh coriander leaves

1 tbsp toasted sesame seeds

50g (2oz) beansprouts

1 tbsp Hoisin sauce

1 tbsp soy sauce

salt and freshly ground black pepper

to serve

boiled rice

soy sauce

Chickpea and Spinach Curry with Flatbread

Vegetarian dishes form a large part of the southern Indian diet, and this one is particularly tasty.

Serves 4

6 tbsp sunflower oil

1 onion, thinly sliced

2 garlic cloves, crushed

2 tbsp grated fresh root ginger

2 green chillies, finely chopped

2 tbsp Madras curry powder

600ml (1 pint) vegetable stock

1 x 200g (7oz) tin chopped tomatoes

225g (8oz) baby new potatoes, halved

1 x 400g (14oz) tin of chickpeas, rinsed

225g (8oz) baby spinach leaves

salt and freshly ground black pepper

for the flatbreads

6 tbsp Greek yoghurt

1 egg, lightly beaten

225g (8oz) self-raising flour

2 tbsp chopped fresh coriander

to serve

25g (1oz) butter

Step one Heat 2 tablespoons of oil in a pan with a lid and sauté the onion for 5 minutes until softened and lightly golden. Stir in the garlic, ginger and half the chopped chillies, and cook for a further minute. Add the curry powder, stock, tomatoes and potatoes, cover and bring to the boil, then simmer for 15–20 minutes until the potatoes are tender but still holding their shape.

Step two To make the flatbreads, heat a large non-stick frying pan. Mix 4 tablespoons of the yoghurt with enough warm water to make 120ml (4fl oz), then stir in the beaten egg. Put the flour into a bowl, along with ½ teaspoon salt. Make a well in the centre and add the yoghurt mixture, the remaining chilli and the coriander. Quickly mix to a soft but not sticky dough.

Step three Turn the dough out onto a lightly floured work surface and knead gently for about 30 seconds until smooth. Divide into 4 portions then, using a rolling pin, roll out each piece to an oval shape about 5 mm (¼in) thick.

Step four Add a thin film of oil to the heated pan and cook the flatbreads, in batches, for 4–5 minutes on each side until cooked through and lightly golden. Wrap in a clean tea towel to keep warm and repeat until all are cooked.

Step five Add the chickpeas and spinach to the curry and cook for a further few minutes until heated through, stirring occasionally. Stir in the remaining yoghurt until just warmed through. To serve, spread the warm flatbreads with the butter. Divide the curry into warmed bowls, with the buttered flatbreads on the side.

Flatbreads can be made in minutes, but don't be tempted to make them too far in advance or they will begin to harden.

Spicy Beanburgers

My beanburgers are nutritious, easy to make and delicious. The kids love to prepare them, and can't wait to eat them. If it's a nice day, why not slap 'em on the barbie? Make sure you squeeze as much water as possible out of the spinach, otherwise the burgers may break up when they are cooked.

Step one Heat the oil in a small pan and cook the onion, garlic and chilli for 5 minutes until softened. Squeeze the excess moisture out of the spinach and place in a large bowl. (To get the maximum amount of water out of the spinach, place it in a tea towel and twist into a tight ball.)

Step two Mash the beans well and mix them with the spinach, breadcrumbs, cumin and coriander. Add the onion mixture and mix well. Season to taste and with slightly wet hands, shape into 4 round burgers and pat them dry with kitchen paper.

Step three Grill, or spray with oil and shallow fry, for a few minutes on each side until crisp and golden. Serve in burger buns, served with salad and low-fat yoghurt mixed with fresh chopped herbs, if liked.

Serves 2

1 tbsp vegetable oil

1 small onion, finely chopped

2 garlic cloves

1 small, hot red chilli, finely chopped

100g (4oz) frozen chopped spinach, thawed

1 x 400g (14oz) tin cannellini beans

50g (2oz) fresh white breadcrumbs

1 tsp ground cumin

1 tbsp chopped fresh coriander

salt and freshly ground black pepper

to serve

burger buns

salad

herby low-fat yoghurt dressing

For a video masterclass on chopping an onion, go to
www.mykitchentable.co.uk/videos/choppingonion

Mama's Greek Butter Bean Salad

This is a lovely Greek-style salad that my favourite Greek mum, Mama Tahsia, makes. It's great served outdoors or as part of a barbecue, and is substantial enough for a main course, served with warm pitta bread and a nice glass of chilled white wine.

Serves 4

4 ripe plum tomatoes

2 tbsp chopped fresh mint

1 small garlic clove, roughly chopped

juice of 1 small lemon

3 tbsp olive oil

2 x 420g tins butter beans, drained

75g (3oz) pitted black olives

1 small red onion, thinly sliced

200g (7oz) feta cheese, roughly cubed

salt and freshly ground black pepper

to serve

warm pitta bread (see tip)

Step one Roughly chop one of the tomatoes and place in a liquidizer or mini food-processor, along with half the mint and all the garlic, and whizz until smooth. Add the lemon juice and olive oil and some salt and pepper and whizz again to make a smooth dressing.

Step two Cut the remaining tomatoes into wedges and toss with the butter beans, olives, red onion and feta, then add the dressing. Transfer to serving plates, scatter over the remaining mint and serve with warm pitta bread.

For crispy pitta, warm them over a barbecue or under the grill then split them in half. Brush the split sides with a little herb oil (mix oil with chopped herbs and seasoning) and return to the heat – but not too close to the hot coals if you're using the barbie – cut-side down to the heat for 2–3 minutes until crisp and golden.

Root Vegetable and Nut Crumble

This is a real winter-warmer dish that even non-vegetarians will love as it's satisfying, too.

Step one Cut the potatoes, carrots, parsnips, butternut squash and swede into 2.5cm (1in) chunks. Melt the butter in a large saucepan, add the vegetable chunks and stir. Cover and cook gently for 10 minutes. Meanwhile, preheat the oven to 190°C/375°F/gas 5.

Step two Add the leeks to the vegetables and continue to cook for a further 3–4 minutes until tender. Stir in the flour and cook for a further minute. Gradually stir in the stock, milk and chopped tomatoes. Cover and bring to the boil, then simmer for 10 minutes until the vegetables are just tender.

Step three For the crumble topping, work the butter into the flour, by hand or in a food-processor, until the mixture resembles coarse breadcrumbs. Stir in the grated cheese, nuts and seeds.

Step four Remove the vegetables from the heat, stir in the parsley and season to taste. Spoon the mixture into a shallow 2.4 litre (4 pint) ovenproof dish and spoon on the topping. Bake for 30 minutes or until golden and bubbling.

Serves 6

175g (6oz) potatoes,

175g (6oz) carrots

175g (6oz) parsnips

175g (6oz) seeded butternut squash

175g (6oz) swede

25g (1oz) butter

2 leeks, sliced

50g (2oz) wholemeal flour

300ml (10fl oz) vegetable stock

150ml (5fl oz) milk

1 x 200g (7oz) tin chopped tomatoes

1 tbsp chopped fresh parsley leaves

salt and freshly ground black pepper

for the crumble

110g (4oz) butter

175g (6oz) plain wholemeal flour

100g (4oz) Cheddar, coarsely grated

75g (3oz) mixed nuts (brazils, almonds and cashews), shelled and coarsely chopped

1 tbsp sunflower seeds

1 tbsp sesame seeds

Cheese 'n' Onion Tarte Tatin

We've done it with apples, we've done it with pears, now do it with onions and watch it disappear. Nothing ever tasted this good upside down.

Serves 4

1 tbsp olive oil

25g (1oz) butter

3 large red onions, thinly sliced

2 tbsp dark muscovado sugar

1 tbsp balsamic vinegar

120g (4½oz) Cheddar, grated

115g (4oz) shortcrust pastry, thawed if frozen

to serve

mixed salad

Step one Preheat the oven to 200°C/400°F/gas 6. Heat the oil and the butter in a large frying pan and cook the onions, stirring occasionally, for 5–8 minutes until softened. Stir in the sugar and vinegar and cook for a further 2 minutes until the sugar has dissolved. Spoon the onions into a 20cm (8in) ovenproof pie dish or sandwich-cake tin. Reserve 25g (1oz) of the cheese and sprinkle the rest over the onions.

Step two Roll the pastry out to a circle slightly larger than the dish, then press it lightly over the cheese, tucking down the sides. Prick gently with a fork and bake for 25 minutes or until the pastry is golden and the filling bubbles up round the edge.

Step three Leave the dish to cool for a few minutes, then set a serving plate on top and invert. While the dish is still warm, sprinkle over the reserved cheese, cut it into wedges and serve with mixed salad.

Griddled Peaches and Mint Feta Cheese Salad

Fruit and cheese don't have to be left until after the meal – serve them as part of your main course in this dee-lish salad. As a change from feta, you could try using low-fat firm cheese, such as reduced-fat Cheddar, or some cottage cheese and rye crackers.

Step one Use half the oil to brush a ridged griddle pan or a frying pan and heat until slightly smoking. Toss the peaches or nectarines in the lime juice. Place flesh-side down onto the griddle and cook for 2–3 minutes until charred.

Step two In a large bowl toss together the remaining oil and lime juice, and the lime zest, salad leaves, onion, sugarsnaps and mint.

Step three Divide the salad between four bowls or serving plates. Scatter over the fruit and feta cheese. Season with a good scattering of freshly ground black pepper and serve warm.

Serves 4

1 tsp olive oil

4 ripe peaches or nectarines, stoned and cut into wedges

finely grated zest and juice of 1 lime

200g mixed salad leaves

1 small red onion, halved and thinly sliced

150g (5oz) sugarsnaps, halved lengthways

2 tbsp chopped fresh mint

200g (7oz) feta cheese, roughly crumbled

freshly ground black pepper

Marinated Halloumi Cheese with Tang! Tang! Dressing

It might seem like there is a lot of cheese in this recipe but it is a dense, heavy cheese and it will give everyone three thin slices. Serve it with crusty fresh bread to soak up all the lovely juices.

Serves 4

2 tbsp olive oil

1 tsp balsamic vinegar

2 tbsp lemon juice

1 tbsp chopped fresh thyme

750g (1¾lb) Halloumi cheese, cut into 12 slices about 1cm (½in) thick

salt and freshly ground black pepper

for the dressing

5 tbsp extra-virgin olive oil

4 plum tomatoes, skinned, seeded and diced

4 spring onions, thinly sliced

½ small red onion, very finely chopped

2 tbsp chopped fresh flat-leaf parsley

1¼ tbsp balsamic vinegar

½ tsp crushed black peppercorns

50g (2oz) Calamata or other black olives

Step one Turn on the grill or light the barbecue. In a large shallow dish, mix together the olive oil, vinegar, lemon juice, thyme and some salt and pepper. Add the cheese slices, turn once or twice in the mixture and leave to marinate at room temperature for up to 1 hour.

Step two When you are ready to start cooking the cheese, mix together all the ingredients for the dressing and add the Calamata olives.

Step three Lift the cheese slices out of the marinade, saving the marinade that's left in the bowl for later. Either cook the cheese under a medium grill or barbecue in batches over medium-hot coals for 1½ minutes on each side or until golden.

Step four Stir the marinade left in the bowl into the dressing. Place 3 slices of cheese on to each plate, spoon over the dressing and garnish with a few black olives. Serve with plenty of crusty fresh bread.

Halloumi won't melt during cooking so it's perfect for slapping on the barbecue. It lacks flavour so it needs to be marinated first and then served with a fresh tangy dressing.

Tomato, Feta and Basil Pizza

This quick and easy pizza is great to have ready for the kids to eat when they get home from school. You can spice it up with other low-fat toppings: try par-boiling courgettes and adding them along with some caramelized onions. When the pizza is cooked, scatter with fresh basil leaves.

Step one Preheat the oven to 220°C/425°F/gas 7, putting a large baking sheet inside to heat at the same time. Mix together the pizza-base mix, herbs and water to form a soft dough. Knead lightly on a lightly floured surface until the dough is smooth. Roll out to about a 25cm (10in) circle.

Step two Lift the pizza circle onto the preheated baking sheet and scatter over the tomatoes, onion and feta. Season and bake for 20 minutes until golden. Scatter over the basil leaves to garnish.

You could use some fresh peppery rocket instead of basil as a garnish.

Serves 4

1 x 145g pack pizza-base mix

2 tbsp roughly chopped fresh mixed herbs (e.g. basil, rosemary, flat-leaf parsley)

100ml (3½ fl oz) hand-hot water

2 plum tomatoes, cut into wedges

8 firm vine-ripened tomatoes, cut into chunks

120g (4oz) cherry tomatoes, halved

1 red onion, cut into thin wedges

75g (3oz) feta cheese, crumbled

salt and freshly ground black pepper

to garnish

fresh basil leaves

Gratin of Penne with Spinach and Tomatoes

This recipe is easy enough for everyday eating, but good enough to serve to friends. If you haven't got time to make a cheese sauce, simply replace with a tub of mascarpone cheese and a couple of handfuls of freshly grated Parmesan.

Serves 4

275g (10oz) penne pasta

450ml (12fl oz) shop-bought cheese sauce

4 tbsp single cream or crème fraîche

a knob of butter, plus extra for greasing

225g (8oz) baby-leaf spinach

2 plum tomatoes, skinned, seeded and cut into strips

4 tbsp freshly grated Parmesan cheese

2 tbsp dried white breadcrumbs, from a packet

salt and freshly ground black pepper

to serve

lightly dressed mixed green salad

Step one Preheat the oven to 190°C/375°F/gas 5. Plunge the penne into a large pan of boiling salted water; stir once, then cook for 8–10 minutes until almost but not quite al dente, as it will finish cooking in the oven.

Step two While the pasta is cooking, place the cheese sauce in a pan, add the cream and heat gently. Melt the butter in a small pan, add the spinach and season to taste, then quickly sauté until wilted. Drain well in a sieve, then squeeze dry.

Step three Butter a shallow ovenproof dish. Drain the pasta, then return it to the pan and fold in the cheese sauce, spinach and tomato strips. Season to taste and tip into the prepared dish.

Step four Mix together the Parmesan and breadcrumbs and scatter over the pasta. Bake for about 20 minutes until the top is crisp and golden. Serve at once, with a lightly dressed salad.

Pecorino Tart with Tarragon Crust

This stunning tart has such a delicious flavour, I just serve it with a classic rocket and cherry-tomato salad for an elegant supper, and any leftovers are delicious served cold.

Step one Preheat the oven to 200°C/400°F/gas 6. Put the flour in a food-processor, add the salt, butter, tarragon and chilli flakes and whizz until the mixture forms fine crumbs. Pour in 3 tablespoons of very cold water and pulse again to form a firm dough. You may need a little more or less water.

Step two Roll the dough out on a floured surface and use to line a 23cm (9in) loose-bottomed tart tin. Rest the pastry case for 5 minutes, if possible. Prick the base, fill with crumpled foil and bake for 10 minutes. Remove the tin from the oven, and reduce the oven to 180°C/350°F/gas 4. Remove the foil from the tart.

Step three Beat together the cream and eggs until they are well blended. Stir in the pecorino and pour into the tart case. Bake for 25 minutes until just set. Carefully remove the tart from the tin and cut into slices. Serve warm with a rocket and tomato salad.

Parmesan makes a good substitute for pecorino. If you have time, chill the pastry case in the freezer for 5 minutes before baking blind – it sets and rests the pastry and helps prevent shrinkage during cooking.

Serves 6 as a main course, or 8 as a starter

300g (11oz) plain flour

½ tsp salt

150g (5oz) chilled butter, diced

2 tbsp roughly chopped fresh tarragon

½ tsp dried chilli flakes

450ml (¾ pint) double cream

2 large eggs, plus 2 yolks

100g (4oz) freshly grated pecorino cheese

to serve

rocket and tomato salad

Blackened Cajun Salmon with Lime Aïoli

Salmon is very reasonably priced these days, and for the best flavour look out for wild Alaskan or organic varieties. I find it a very versatile fish and, because it's got a naturally high fat content, it's perfect for roasting or grilling.

Serves 4

2 tsp Cajun seasoning

4 x 150g (5oz) salmon fillets, skin on, scaled and boned

2 tbsp extra-virgin olive oil

for the lime aioli

3 tbsp mayonnaise

1 garlic clove, crushed

1 lime

salt and freshly ground black pepper

Step one Preheat the oven to 180°C/350°F/gas 4. Spoon the Cajun seasoning onto a flat plate and use to dust the salmon fillets, shaking off any excess. Heat an ovenproof frying pan or griddle pan. Add half the olive oil and sear the salmon, skin-side down, for 30 seconds, then turn over and cook for 1 minute. Transfer to the oven and roast for 6 minutes or until tender but still very moist in the middle.

Step two Meanwhile, make the lime aïoli. Put the mayonnaise in a bowl and beat in the remaining olive oil and the garlic. Add a light grating of lime zest, then cut the lime in half and add a squeeze of the juice from one half. Season to taste and mix well to combine.

Step three Arrange the salmon on plates and add a tablespoon of the lime aïoli by the side of each. Cut the remaining lime half into quarters and serve with the salmon.

For a video masterclass on filleting a salmon, go to
www.mykitchentable.co.uk/videos/filleting

Cod Kebab Zingers with Salsa Tagliatelle

My lively lime marinade firms up the fish nicely, keeping it on the skewers once it's cooked rather than in the bottom of the grill pan. To add a kick to your pasta, add one small fresh, seeded and chopped chilli – but remember that some chillies are hotter than others, so check them out before using.

Step one Preheat the grill to high. In a large bowl mix together the lime zest, half the lime juice and half the oil, then stir in the cubed cod. Season with salt and pepper and set to one side to marinate for 5 minutes.

Step two Thread the cod cubes onto 6 skewers, season and grill for 8–10 minutes, turning once, until tender and golden.

Step three Meanwhile, cook the tagliatelle according to packet instructions in a large pan of boiling, salted water, adding the green beans 3 minutes before the end of the cooking time. Drain. Heat the remaining oil in the pan and fry the tomatoes and red onion for 2 minutes.

Step four Toss the pasta into the pan with the green beans, parsley or coriander and remaining lime juice. Season to taste and serve with the fish kebabs.

Serves 3

grated zest of 1 lime

juice of 2 limes

2 tbsp olive oil

450g (1lb) skinned thick cod fillets, cubed

225g (8oz) tagliatelle

150g (15oz) fine green beans, trimmed

200g (7oz) cherry tomatoes, halved

1 small red onion, finely chopped

1 tbsp chopped fresh parsley or coriander

salt and freshly ground black pepper

Spiced Smoked Mackerel Pilaf with Onion Raita and Minty Yoghurt Dressing

This dish is amazingly good for you, without compromising on taste. It's delicious served with mango chutney.

Serves 4

250g (9oz) brown basmati rice

1 tbsp olive oil

1 onion, sliced

1 garlic clove

3 tsp root ginger

2 cardamom pods

½ tsp ground cumin

½ tsp cayenne

½ tsp turmeric

1 bay leaf

450ml (¾ pint) vegetable stock

250g (9oz) smoked mackerel, flaked

75g (3oz) peas

salt and freshly ground black pepper

fresh coriander leaves, to garnish

for the onion raita

1 red onion

lime juice, to taste

pinch of cayenne

salt

for the minty yoghurt dressing

1 tbsp fresh mint

100g (4oz) low-fat natural yoghurt

Step one Soak the rice in cold water for about 30 minutes. Meanwhile, make the raita and the dressing. For the raita, thinly slice the red onion, place it in a small bowl, add the lime juice and cayenne and mix together. Season with salt, cover and set aside. For the dressing, finely chop the fresh mint and mix together with the yoghurt, then cover and chill.

Step two Prepare the ingredients for the pilaf. Rinse and drain the rice in a sieve. Crush the garlic clove, grate the ginger and lightly crush the cardamom pods.

Step three Heat the oil in a deep sauté pan, add the onion and cook for about 5 minutes, until the onion is lightly coloured. Add the garlic, ginger and spices. Cook for 1 minute, then stir in the rice. Add the bay leaf and stock and bring to the boil. Reduce the heat, cover and simmer very gently for 20 minutes.

Step three Fork the flaked mackerel into the rice, along with the peas, cover and turn the heat off. Leave the pilaf for about 5–10 minutes so that the rice is dried out and really tender, and the mackerel has heated through. Scatter with coriander and serve with the raita, dressing and some mango chutney.

I prefer to use plain smoked mackerel as the peppered variety is overly peppery. You could use white rice, but brown rice has a much better flavour and is a good source of fibre. Instead of the raita and dressing you could top each portion with a soft poached egg and a twist of pepper.

Smoked Haddock Rarebits

At last, it's easy to buy good haddock. For many years it seemed that the only available smoked haddock was dyed fluorescent yellow and chemically treated to taste of smoke. Now it's easy to pick out the good stuff because it's not dyed. Adding some crisp bacon at the end would be a nice touch, and gives an interesting combination of flavours.

Step one Place the haddock in a sauté pan and pour in the milk. Set over a medium heat and bring to the boil. Reduce the heat to a gentle simmer, cover and cook for about 5–6 minutes. Remove the fish from the pan and cool slightly, then flake into chunks.

Step two Meanwhile, preheat the grill. Toast the bread on both sides. Mix the cheese sauce with the mustard, Worcestershire sauce and chives, and season to taste. With a large metal spoon, fold in the haddock and tomatoes.

Step three Divide the cheesy fish mixture between the toasted bread and scatter with the Parmesan. Grill until hot, bubbling and golden brown. Serve immediately, with steamed spinach.

Serves 4

450–500g (1lb–1lb 2oz) smoked haddock fillet

250ml (8fl oz) milk

4 slices from a small white bloomer

1 x 350g (12oz) tub fresh cheese sauce

2 tsp Dijon or wholegrain mustard

splash of Worcestershire sauce

1 tbsp snipped fresh chives

8 cherry tomatoes, halved

2 tbsp freshly grated Parmesan

salt and freshly ground black pepper

French-style Roasted Cod

This beautifully easy, rustic-style dish is packed with flavour. Serve it at the table so your guests see it, still sizzling, in its roasting tin.

Serves 4

450g (1lb) floury potatoes, such as Maris Piper, peeled and cubed

1 whole garlic bulb

4 plum tomatoes

4 sprigs of rosemary

3 tbsp olive oil

4 x 150g (5oz) thick boneless cod fillets, skin on

4 tbsp white wine

salt and freshly ground black pepper

to garnish

handful of fresh basil leaves

Step one Preheat the oven to 220°C/425°F/gas 7. Cook the potatoes in a large pan of boiling water for 10 minutes until almost tender and starting to crumble slightly around the edges. Remove from the heat and drain well.

Step two Transfer the potatoes to a large roasting tin. Break up the garlic bulb and nestle the cloves, unpeeled, between the potatoes. Roughly chop the tomatoes and scatter over the top, along with the rosemary. Season generously, then drizzle over 2 tbsp of the olive oil. Roast for 15 minutes.

Step three Add the cod fillets to the roasting tin, allowing them to rest on top of the vegetables. Drizzle the remaining oil over the top, season the fish and continue roasting for 5 minutes. Splash in the wine and cook for a further 5 minutes until the fish is just cooked. Tear over the basil leaves and serve straight from the dish. Remember to remind your guests that they'll need to peel the garlic cloves before eating them.

Roasted Parma-wrapped Halibut with Sage Lentils

I love dishes where you can just wrap things up and pop them in the oven while you make a simple accompaniment. This recipe fits the bill and makes a very stylish meal in minutes. You could use salmon or haddock instead of halibut.

Step one Preheat the oven to 220°C/425°F/gas 7 and place a baking sheet on the top shelf. Chop the carrot and celery into small dice and finely chop the onion. Alternatively, cut the carrot and celery into large pieces, and blitz them in a food-processor for 5 seconds, then quarter the onion, add it to the other vegetables and blitz again for another 5 seconds.

Step two Heat half the oil in a sauté pan, add the vegetables and cook over a medium heat for 5 minutes. Add the garlic and sage and continue cooking for a further couple of minutes. Stir in the mustard, tomatoes, lentils, stock, sugar and the remaining oil and season well. Bring to the boil, reduce the heat and simmer gently for about 7 minutes.

Step three Wrap a slice of Parma ham around each halibut fillet, and place on the hot baking sheet. Roast for about 10 minutes, until the fish is cooked through.

Step four Stir the parsley into the lentils, check the seasoning, and divide the lentils between four warmed plates. Top with the Parma-wrapped halibut fillets and serve.

Serves 4

1 carrot
1 celery stick
1 onion
2 tbsp olive oil
1 garlic clove, crushed
6 fresh sage leaves, chopped
½ tsp English mustard
1 x 200g (7oz) tin chopped tomatoes
1 x 410g (14½oz) tin lentils, drained
150ml (¼ pint) vegetable stock
pinch of caster sugar
4 slices Parma ham or similar
4 x 150–175g (5–6oz) halibut fillets
1–2 tbsp chopped fresh parsley
salt and freshly ground black pepper

For more recipes from My Kitchen Table, sign up for our newsletter at www.mykitchentable.co.uk/newsletter

Warm Salmon Tart

You can make the pastry case for this tart up to 24 hours in advance, but if you're short on time you can use shop-bought pastry or a ready-made shortcrust pastry case instead.

Serves 4–6

225g (8oz) salmon
fillet or cutlets

2 eggs, plus
2 egg yolks

150ml (¼ pint)
double cream

2 tbsp snipped
fresh chives

salt and freshly ground
black pepper

for the pastry

100g (4oz) plain flour,
plus extra for dusting

50g (2oz) unsalted
butter, chilled and
cut into cubes

1 egg

1–2 tbsp ice-cold
water

to serve

lightly dressed fresh
green salad (optional)

Step one To make the pastry, put the flour in a food-processor, add a pinch of salt and the butter and blend together briefly until the mixture resembles fine breadcrumbs, then tip into a bowl. Separate the egg and set aside the unbeaten egg white. Gently mix the egg yolk into the flour mixture with enough of the ice-cold water for pastry to just come together. Knead gently on a lightly floured surface for a few seconds to give a smooth dough. Wrap in clingfilm and chill for about 10 minutes before rolling (or up to 1 hour if time allows). Preheat the oven to 180°C/350°F/gas 4.

Step two On a lightly floured surface, roll out the pastry as thinly as possible. Use it to line a loose-bottomed 20cm (8in) fluted tart tin that is about 4cm (1½in) deep. Chill again for 10 minutes to allow the pastry to rest.

Step three Prick the pastry base with a fork, then line with a circle of non-stick baking paper (crumple it first to make it easier to handle). Fill with baking beans or dried pulses and bake for about 15 minutes until the case looks 'set', but not coloured. Carefully remove the paper, then brush the inside with the reserved unbeaten egg white to form a seal. Place in the oven for a further 5 minutes or until the base is firm to the touch and the sides are lightly coloured.

Step four Reduce the oven temperature to 160°C/325°F/gas 3. Cut the salmon into 2cm (¾in) pieces, discarding all the skin and any bones. Whisk the eggs and yolks in a bowl, beat in the cream and chives and season. Scatter the salmon in the bottom of the pastry case, then pour over the cream mixture. Bake for 20–25 minutes or until the tart is just set but still slightly wobbly in the middle. Serve warm, with fresh green salad, if liked.

Monkfish on Crispy Potato Cakes

A perfect combination of flavours and textures for you to enjoy.

Step one Wrap each monkfish fillet in 2–3 slices of smoked pancetta, overlapping the edges slightly. Tie in a couple of places with some fine string and set aside. Preheat the oven to 200°C/400°F/gas 6. Pour the stock into a small pan, add the wine and cream and boil until reduced to 85ml (3fl oz). Set aside.

Step two Melt half the butter in an ovenproof frying pan, add the monkfish, seam-side up, and fry for 1–1½ minutes until golden brown. Turn over, transfer to the oven and roast for 10 minutes.

Step three Meanwhile, prepare the potato cakes. Finely grate the potatoes, by hand or in a food-processor. Working with small handfuls at a time, squeeze out as much excess liquid from them as you can. Put into a bowl, fork to separate into strands and mix in the shallots, egg, flour, a scant ½ tsp salt and some pepper.

Step four Pour the oil into a frying pan so that it is 5mm (¼in) deep, and set over a medium heat. Divide the potato mixture into 4 then shape each portion into thin circles 7.5cm (3in) wide. Fry in the oil for 3 minutes on each side until golden brown and crisp on the outside and cooked through in the centre. Drain briefly on kitchen paper and keep warm.

Step five Remove the monkfish from the oven, turn the oven off, but leave the potato cakes inside. Transfer the fish to a plate and remove the string. Add the reduced chicken stock to the frying pan and bring to the boil, rubbing the base of the pan with a wooden spoon. Whisk in the remaining butter, stir in the parsley and season with a little salt and pepper. Put the potato cakes into the centre of warmed plates and place the monkfish on top. Spoon around the sauce, and serve with a green vegetable.

Serves 2

2 x 175g (6oz) monkfish fillets, trimmed

4–6 long, thin slices smoked pancetta

300ml (10fl oz) chicken stock

85ml (3fl oz) dry white wine

3 tbsp double cream

25g (1oz) butter

the leaves from 1 large sprig of parsley, chopped

salt and freshly ground black pepper

for the crispy potato cakes

2 potatoes, 100–150g (4–5oz) each, peeled

2 small shallots, finely chopped

1 egg, beaten

1 slightly rounded tbsp self-raising flour

sunflower oil, for shallow frying

to serve

a green vegetable

Salmon and Spinach Fishcakes with Beetroot and Horseradish Relish

Use fresh beetroot if in season – roast or boil them leaving at least 5mm (½in) of stalk at the top because, if too closely trimmed, they will 'bleed', losing colour and some of their flavour. These fishcakes are best served simply with lemon wedges and a watercress salad.

Serves 4

450g (1lb) skinless, boneless salmon fillet

2 tbsp olive oil

450g (1lb) floury potatoes, peeled and quartered

1.75 litres (3 pints) boiling, salted water

175g (6oz) young leaf spinach, washed

grated zest of ½ lemon

1 tbsp capers, rinsed and finely chopped

2–3 tbsp plain flour

25g (1oz) butter

salt and freshly ground black pepper

for the relish

250g (9oz) cooked beetroot

1 heaped tsp horseradish sauce

1 tbsp chopped fresh parsley

1 tbsp snipped fresh chives

2 heaped tbsp Greek yoghurt or crème fraîche

2–3 tsp lemon juice

Step one Preheat the oven to 190°C/375°F/gas 5. Drizzle the salmon with 2 teaspoons of the oil, season, cover with foil and bake for 15–20 minutes, until cooked through. Cool, then flake the fish into pieces. You could use a fork to do this.

Step two Meanwhile, cook the potatoes in the boiling water for 15 minutes until tender. Put the spinach in a sauté pan with 2 tablespoons of cold water, cover and cook for 2–3 minutes, until the spinach is wilted. Drain well, cool and roughly chop. Drain the potatoes thoroughly and mash until smooth.

Step three In a large bowl mix combine the mashed potato, salmon, chopped spinach, lemon zest and capers. Season well. Divide the mixture into eight equal portions and shape into patties. Cover and chill while you prepare the relish.

Step four Coarsely grate the beetroot, and add the horseradish, parsley, chives and yoghurt or crème fraîche. Season, mix well, and add lemon juice to taste.

Step five Lightly coat the fishcakes in the flour. Heat half the butter and 1 tbsp of the oil in a large frying pan. Add four of the fishcakes and cook for about 4 minutes on each side, until golden brown. Remove from the pan and keep warm. Heat the remaining butter and oil in the pan and cook the remaining fishcakes in the same way. Serve with a watercress salad, lemon wedges and the beetroot and horseradish relish.

These fishcakes can be made in advance and freeze well. You can also use fresh horseradish if available, instead of the ready-made sauce.

Glazed Monkfish Skewers with Udon Noodles

These succulent monkfish skewers are perfect for cooking on a barbecue; fish does tend to break up slightly on the barbecue though, so it is a good idea to buy a hinged grill for easy turning. Thick Japanese rice noodles are a satisfying accompaniment.

Step one Thread the monkfish cubes onto 8 skewers. (If you use wooden skewers you'll need to soak them for 20 minutes beforehand.)

Step two Mix together the soy sauce, tomato purée, vinegar, lime juice, honey, fish sauce, chilli oil and coriander, then brush the mixture over the kebabs.

Step three Cook the skewers over hot coals on the barbie, or under a preheated hot grill, for about 6–8 minutes, turning frequently, until the fish is cooked through and a little charred.

Step four Meanwhile, run the noodles under hot water to separate out a little, then steam them over a pan of boiling water with the pak choy for 3–4 minutes. Dish out the noodles onto plates and serve the monkfish skewers piled on top.

Serves 4

500g (1lb 2oz) cubed monkfish, or any firm white fish

2 tbsp soy sauce

1 tbsp tomato purée

1 tbsp vinegar

juice of 1 lime

1 tbsp clear honey

½ tsp Thai fish sauce

½ tsp chilli oil

1 tbsp chopped fresh coriander

250g (9oz) udon noodles

4 heads pak choy, roughly chopped

Pan-seared Mumbai Mackerel with Waldorf Salad

The perfect partner for these spiced mackerel fillets is a crisp, classic salad lightly dressed in crème fraîche and mayonnaise. Get the fishmonger to fillet and bone the mackerel for you. Use a fresh, good-quality curry powder, it makes a world of difference.

Serves 4

4 medium mackerel, filleted and boned

2 tbsp mild curry powder

2 tbsp olive oil

a few knobs of butter

salt and freshly ground black pepper

for the Waldorf salad

¼ head white cabbage

2 small eating apples, such as Cox's orange pippins, cored and diced

2 celery sticks, sliced

3 spring onions, sliced

50g (2oz) toasted walnuts, chopped

1 heaped tbsp crème fraîche

1 heaped tbsp mayonnaise

to serve

lemon wedges

Step one Prepare the Waldorf salad first. Shred the cabbage as finely as possible or use the large grating disc/blade on your food-processor. Place in a large bowl, add the apples, celery, onions and walnuts and toss. Add the crème fraîche and mayonnaise, season and mix well to coat everything nicely.

Step two Season each mackerel fillet with a good dusting of curry powder, salt and pepper. Heat the olive oil in a large frying pan over a medium-high heat. Add a knob of butter (about a teaspoonful) followed immediately by the spiced mackerel fillets, placed skin-side down, and cook for about 1 minute until the skin is crisp. Flip the fillets over and cook for a further 30–60 seconds, until cooked through. You may need to cook the fish in batches, in which case keep the first batch warm while you cook the rest.

Step three Divide the Waldorf salad between four plates and serve the mackerel fillets criss-crossed on top, with lemon wedges to squeeze over.

Pan-fried Plaice with Crispy Bacon

The combination of fish and bacon may not be an obvious one, but it really is a winner. Use dry-cured streaky bacon, if possible, or pancetta, the Italian equivalent.

Step one Heat a large, heavy-based frying pan and preheat the grill. Grill the bacon for a minute or so on each side until crisp. Drain on kitchen paper and allow to crisp up completely.

Step two Meanwhile, place the seasoned flour on a plate and lightly dust two of the fish fillets with it, shaking off any surplus. Add a knob of the butter to the pan and, when it foams, add the floured plaice flesh-side down. Cook for 2 minutes until lightly golden, then turn over and cook for a further 1–2 minutes, depending on the thickness of the fillets. Transfer to a serving plate and keep warm.

Step three Add another knob of butter to the pan. Lightly dust and cook the remaining plaice fillets as before. Using scissors, snip the bacon rashers over all the fish, then keep warm.

Step four Wipe out the pan. Add the remaining butter, allowing it to melt over a moderate heat. When it turns to light brown foam, quickly add the herbs and a squeeze of lemon juice, swirling to combine. Spoon this mixture over the plaice and bacon, then serve with crushed new potatoes.

Serves 2

6 thin, rindless streaky bacon rashers

25g (1oz) seasoned plain flour

4 × 100g (4oz) plaice fillets, skinned

50g (2oz) unsalted butter

1 tbsp chopped mixed herbs, such as parsley, chives and tarragon

½ lemon, pips removed

salt and freshly ground black pepper

to serve

crushed new potatoes

Gambas Pil Pil

The first time I had this was under a hot sun in Spain with the sand between my toes. If possible, use fresh prawns, but remove the shells before cooking as otherwise it gets a bit messy. The quality of the paprika you use in this dish makes all the difference – you'll find wonderful smoked paprika in the gourmet foods area of larger supermarkets.

Serves 4

300g (10oz) unsalted butter

3 garlic cloves, crushed

1 tbsp smoked paprika

1.5kg (3lb) raw tiger prawns (64–80 in total), peeled and veins removed, but tails intact

2 tbsp chopped fresh flat-leaf parsley

salt and freshly ground black pepper

to garnish

lemon wedges

to serve

fresh crusty bread

Step one Put the butter in a pan, along with the garlic and paprika and season generously and heat until the butter is just starting to foam. Tip in the prawns – stand back as they may spit. Cook the prawns for 2–3 minutes or until they have changed to a pinky-orange colour and are tender and cooked through.

Step two Spoon the prawns and butter mixture into serving bowls and scatter over the parsley. Garnish with the lemon wedges and serve with plenty of crusty bread. You may like to have a finger bowl or some napkins at the ready!

Jalapeño Tiger Prawn Ginger Skewers

I first made these in Key West, Florida, overlooking the waters of the Gulf of Mexico. The locals were so impressed that their barbie bar now has them on its menu. I use jalapeño chillies for this dish because they have a delicate flavour. Try to get a variety of colours – red, green and yellow. You will need to soak the wooden skewers for 20 minutes before using them.

Step one Light the barbecue or turn on the grill. Slit open the chillies from top to tail, taking care to leave the stalks intact. Scrape out the seeds. Divide the shredded basil and chopped ginger between the chillies and generously season the inside of the chillies.

Step two Shell the prawns, leaving the tail section intact. Place a whole prawn inside each chilli, leaving the tail poking out of the pointed end. Smear a little butter on top of each prawn, then squeeze the chillies shut to enclose the prawns.

Step three Thread three chillies, alternating the colours, onto two parallel soaked wooden skewers so that the chillies look like the rungs of a ladder. Repeat to make 8 ladders.

Step four Cook the chillies over fairly hot coals or under a hot grill for about 5 minutes, turning frequently, until they are softened and a little charred, and the prawns are cooked through. Serve with wedges of lemon or lime. Delicious.

Serves 4

12 red jalapeño chillies

12 green jalapeño chillies

12 fresh basil leaves, finely shredded

4cm (1½ in) piece fresh root ginger, peeled and finely chopped

24 raw tiger prawns

a knob of butter

salt and freshly ground black pepper

to serve

lemon or lime wedges

Coconut-and-Cumin-spiced Prawns with Chapatis

Buy large cooked, peeled North Atlantic prawns for this curry. And if you are buying them frozen, you will need to buy a few more, as they lose quite a lot of their weight when they defrost. About 550g (1¼ lb) will give you 450g (1lb) once they have thawed out.

Serves 4

3 tbsp sunflower oil

1 medium onion, finely chopped

2.5cm (1in) fresh root ginger, peeled and finely grated

3 garlic cloves, crushed

1 tsp sambal oelek

4 tsp hot paprika

2 tbsp garam masala or korma curry paste

2 tsp lemon juice

150ml (5fl oz) hot water

1 × 200g (7oz) can chopped tomatoes

450g (1lb) cooked peeled prawns

50g (2oz) creamed coconut, chopped

1 × 20g (3/4oz) packet fresh coriander, chopped

salt and cayenne pepper

to serve

1 packet ready-made chapatis

Step one Heat the oil in a large frying pan, add the onion, ginger, garlic and sambal oelek and fry for 3–4 minutes until soft and very lightly browned. Add the paprika and garam masala and fry for 2 minutes. Then add the lemon juice and water and simmer for a further 2 minutes.

Step two Add the tomatoes and prawns and simmer for about 2 minutes. Stir in the creamed coconut and cook for a further minute. Season to taste, stir in the coriander and serve with warmed chapatis.

I've used the Indonesian sambal oelek for this dish, but you could use any chilli paste.

Seared Squid with Citrus Mango Salad

The secret of lovely tender squid is to not overcook it. Once it turns white and starts to curl up – hey presto! – it's cooked. It's best to get your frying pan really hot before you start to sear the squid; if you're in an al fresco mood, sear it over hot coals.

Step one In a bowl mix together the fish sauce, soy sauce and lime juice, and toss in the coriander. Slit the squid tubes down one side and open out flat. Score the inside flesh in a criss-cross pattern.

Step two Heat the oil in a frying pan and stir-fry the squid and onion for 4–5 minutes (the squid will curl up and roll itself when cooked). Remove from the heat and pour over the coriander mixture. Toss well to coat.

Step three Arrange the salad leaves and mango slices on individual serving plates, place the seared squid on top and spoon over the remaining juices. Serve immediately.

Serves 4

1 tsp Thai fish sauce

1 tbsp soy sauce

juice of ½ lime

2 tbsp chopped fresh coriander

12 small squid tubes, thawed if frozen

1 tbsp olive oil

1 small red onion, diced

120g mixed salad leaves

1 ripe mango, skinned, stoned and thinly sliced

Summer Seafood Marinara

This recipe is perfect for lazy summer evenings when you want something light.

Serves 4

1.75kg (4lb) mussels and/or clams

4 tbsp dry white wine

450g (1lb) spaghetti

4 tbsp olive oil

2 garlic cloves, very finely chopped

1 medium-hot red chilli, seeded and finely chopped

225g (8oz) peeled raw prawns

300ml (½ pint) passata rustica

a handful of basil leaves, torn into pieces

2 tbsp chopped fresh flat-leaf parsley

salt and freshly ground black pepper

Step one To clean the mussels, wash them under cold running water and discard any that are open and won't close when lightly squeezed or tapped on the work surface. Then pull out the fibrous beards from between the closed shells. The clams just need to be washed.

Step two Put the mussels and/or clams in a pan and pour in the wine. Cover tightly and cook over a high heat for a few minutes, shaking the pan occasionally until all the shellfish have opened; discard any that do not open. Strain through a sieve, reserving 150ml (5 fl oz) of the cooking liquor, and discard the grit. Take the meat out of the shells and set aside.

Step three Put the spaghetti into a pan of boiling, salted water, stir once, then cook for 10–12 minutes until al dente or according to the packet instructions.

Step four Meanwhile, heat the oil in a heavy-based frying pan, add the garlic and chilli, then sauté for 20 seconds. Tip in the prawns and sauté for another minute or so until just sealed. Pour in the passata and add the reserved shellfish cooking liquor. Bring to a gentle simmer, then stir in the cooked shellfish plus the basil and parsley. Season to taste and allow to just warm through.

Step five When the pasta is cooked, drain and return it to the pan. Pour in the seafood sauce and fold together until well combined. Serve immediately.

KITCHEN TABLE

For a video masterclass on cleaning mussels, go to www.mykitchentable.co.uk/videos/cleaningmussels

Spaghetti with Clams, Pimento and Capers

The sweet, piquant red peppers known as pimentos are perfect in this dish. Use any leftovers to liven up a salad, or drain well on kitchen paper and fill them with hummus.

Step one Cook the spaghetti in a large pan of boiling salted water for 8–10 minutes, or as per packet instructions, until al dente (cooked but retaining some bite).

Step two Meanwhile, heat the oil in a large frying pan or sauté pan and gently fry the salad onions for 1 minute. Pour in the wine and allow to bubble up, then tip in the clams and simmer, uncovered, for 3 minutes or until all the clams have opened. Discard any that have not, as they are not safe to eat.

Step three Add the pimentos to the pan, along with the lemon zest and juice and the capers, stirring to combine. Season to taste, bearing in mind that capers can be quite salty. Drain the spaghetti and tip into the pan with the clams and mix gently until combined. Divide among warmed serving bowls and scatter over the parsley. Garnish with the lemon wedges and serve.

Serves 4

400g (14oz) spaghetti

2 tbsp olive oil

4 spring onions, trimmed and cut diagonally into 2.5cm (1in) slices

150ml (¼ pint) dry white wine

275g (10oz) fresh clams (amande, palourde or tellini, or a selection of all three types), cleaned

75g (3oz) whole pimentos (from a jar or tin is fine), diced

finely grated zest and juice of 1 lemon

3 tbsp capers, rinsed

2 tbsp chopped fresh flat-leaf parsley

salt and freshly ground black pepper

to garnish

lemon wedges

Seared Scallops with Coriander and Garlic Oil Dressing

I first cooked this on a barbie at the top of Signal Hill in Newfoundland, Canada, with the most amazing icebergs drifting by in the Atlantic Ocean behind me. You may not have quite the same setting when you cook this dish, but the chances are that it will taste every bit as good as mine did. If you buy scallops out of their shells, remember to ask the fishmonger to give you the shells separately.

Serves 4

4 tbsp olive oil, plus extra for brushing

juice of 1 lemon

2 garlic cloves, finely chopped

2 tbsp finely chopped fresh coriander

12 fresh scallops, in their shells

salt and freshly ground black pepper

Step one Light the barbecue or heat a griddle pan. Make the dressing by whisking together the olive oil, lemon juice, garlic and coriander, and season to taste.

Step two Holding the scallops in their shells flat-side up, slide a blade between the shells. Keeping the blade as close to the inside of the top shell as possible, slice the ligaments so that the shells open. Snap off the top shells and remove and discard the black stomach sac and lacy grey edging around the scallops. Cut the scallops away from the bottom shell, then wash the scallops and the bottom shells thoroughly.

Step three Lightly brush the scallops with a little oil and cook over hot coals or in a hot griddle pan for 1 minute on each side until well browned. Return the scallops to the clean bottom shells and drizzle over the dressing. Serve warm.

Mussels in Cider and Crème Fraîche with Salty Home-made Oven Chips

Green-lipped New Zealand mussels are meatier and have a more distinctive flavour than their European counterparts. I like to sprinkle them with herby garlic-butter breadcrumbs and grill them.

Step one Preheat the oven to 220°C/425°F/gas 7. Cook the potatoes whole in boiling water for 10 minutes. Drain and, when cool enough to handle, cut into chunky chips. Place in a bowl, pour over the oil and mix to coat thoroughly. Arrange the chips in a single layer on a large baking sheet, season with sea salt and bake for about 35–40 minutes, until golden brown and crisp.

Step two When the chips have been in the oven for about 20 minutes, start preparing the mussels. Tip them into a clean sink filled with cold water. Discard any with cracked or chipped shells. Give any open ones a sharp tap: if they don't close up tightly, discard them too. Pull out any fibrous beards, rinse off any grit or dirt and set aside in a bowl of clean cold water.

Step three Melt the butter in a pan that's large enough to hold all the mussels and has a tight-fitting lid. Add the leek and shallots and cook over a medium heat for about 3 minutes, until starting to soften. Add the garlic and cook for a further 30 seconds. Drain the mussels and tip them into the pan, then add the cider and bring to the boil. Cover and cook for 3–5 minutes, shaking the pan occasionally, until all the mussels are wide open.

Step four Using a slotted spoon, scoop the mussels into a large serving bowl and cover with a cloth or foil to keep warm. Return the pan to the heat and boil to reduce the cider by half. Stir in the crème fraîche and boil for 30 seconds. Check the seasoning, then pour the liquor over the mussels. Scatter with the parsley and serve immediately with the oven chips.

You could use the blue-black variety of mussels, which are less expensive, for this dish, but go for medium to small mussels, as large ones are not so appetising.

Serves 2

750g (1½ lb) waxy potatoes, washed

2 tbsp sunflower or groundnut oil

flaky sea salt, for the chips

1kg (2¼ lb) live mussels

25g (1oz) butter

1 leek, thinly sliced

2 shallots, thinly sliced

1 garlic clove, crushed

250ml (8fl oz) dry cider

4 tbsp crème fraîche

2 tbsp roughly chopped fresh parsley

salt and freshly ground black pepper

Sinhalese Linguine Prawn Pasta

Sometimes it's the quick and easy meals that are the best, and the ones you return to time and again. This brilliant dish is ready in 20 minutes from start to finish. Try using spaghetti or noodles for a change and if you're not into fish, marinated tofu is delicious instead of prawns.

Serves 4

450g (1lb) linguine

1.75 litres (3 pints)
boiling water, (salted
if preferred)

2 tsp olive oil

½ small onion,
finely chopped

1 garlic clove, crushed

1 tbsp curry paste

1 tbsp chopped
fresh coriander, plus
extra to garnish

1 tbsp chopped
fresh mint

1 tbsp chopped
fresh parsley

225g (8oz) peeled
cooked prawns

grated zest and juice
of 1 lemon

salt and freshly ground
black pepper

Step one Cook the linguine in the boiling water, following the packet cooking instructions. When the pasta is al dente (tender but still offering some resistance when bitten), remove from the heat and drain, reserving 180ml (8 fl oz) of the cooking liquor.

Step two Heat the oil in a large frying pan or wok, add the onion and garlic and fry for a few minutes so they soften but do not colour. Add the curry paste and stir-fry for 20 seconds, then throw in the reserved pasta cooking liquor, all the herbs, prawns and lemon zest. Toss to heat through, then squeeze in the lemon juice. Lightly season.

Step three Toss the cooked pasta with the curried prawn mixture and serve garnished with coriander leaves.

For a video masterclass on making fresh pasta, go to
www.mykitchentable.co.uk/videos/makingpasta

Tandoori-Tikka King Prawns

This isn't a classic Indian dish, it's one that I've brought together in the style of my favourite tandoori and tikka dry-cooked dishes. Serve it with a dollop of raita (or even tzatziki) and a pile of chapatis, all of which are available in supermarkets.

Serves 4

1 garlic clove, crushed

1 tsp ground cumin

½ tsp chilli powder

½ tsp ground turmeric

½ tsp salt

150g natural yoghurt

a few drops of red food colouring (optional)

20 large raw tiger prawns, shells removed but tail sections left intact

to serve

1 lemon, cut into wedges

chapatis

raita (see tip)

Step one Preheat the grill to high, or heat a large, non-stick frying pan. In a large, shallow dish, mix together the garlic, cumin, chilli, turmeric, salt, yoghurt and food colouring, if using. Add the prawns and mix well to coat.

Step two Thread the prawns onto soaked wooden skewers and cook for 5 minutes, turning regularly until the coating is dark red and the prawns are cooked through. Serve with lemon wedges, raita and chapatis.

To make a quick raita, mix together a carton of natural yoghurt with some grated or diced cucumber, a crushed garlic clove, a pinch of salt and sugar and some chopped fresh mint.

Aromatic Pad Thai Chicken

I ate my best Pad Thai while sitting on a very small rickety chair on a Bangkok pavement. The aroma was sensational, with the combination of all those wonderful ingredients.

Serves 4

250g (9oz) dried flat rice noodles

2 tbsp sunflower oil

2 boneless, skinless chicken breasts, cut into 2cm (¾in) strips

1 shallot, finely sliced

2.5cm (1in) root ginger or galangal, finely chopped

1 lemon grass stalk, outer leaves removed and the core finely chopped

1 red bird's-eye chilli, finely chopped

2 kaffir lime leaves, finely shredded

1 garlic clove, finely chopped

4 baby pak choy, quartered

3 tbsp dark soy sauce

2 tbsp Thai fish sauce

juice of 1 lime, plus 1 lime for wedges

2 tbsp sesame oil

3 tbsp chopped, roasted peanuts

a large handful of coriander leaves

Step one Soak the noodles in a large bowl of boiling water for 6 minutes or as per the packet instructions. Heat the oil in a large wok or frying pan and stir fry the chicken over a medium heat for 4–5 minutes until just starting to brown.

Step two Add the shallot to the wok, along with the ginger or galangal, lemon grass, chilli, lime leaves and garlic. Mix well, then tip in the pak choy and stir fry for a further 2 minutes. Pour the soy and fish sauces into the wok and simmer for 4 minutes until the chicken is cooked through and tender. Squeeze over the juice of 1 lime and mix well.

Step three Drain the noodles and tip into the chicken, then toss and stir until well combined. Divide the Pad Thai between warmed serving bowls, drizzle over a little sesame oil, a scattering of peanuts and some coriander. Serve immediately, garnished with lime wedges.

KITCHEN TABLE

For a video masterclass on chopping vegetables, go to www.mykitchentable.co.uk/videos/choppingvegetables

Crispy Chilli Orange Grilled Chicken

When it comes to chicken I'm a thigh man as I think they have the best flavour and are also the most succulent. But do use breast if you prefer, just cook for about 10 minutes longer.

Step one In a large bowl mix together the oil, garlic, sugar and chilli flakes – the amount you use depends on how hot you like your food. Slash the skin of each chicken thigh to help the flavours penetrate, and then add to the bowl along with half the orange wedges. Season generously and mix to coat all the chicken pieces. Cover with clingfilm and set aside for at least 15 minutes to allow the flavours to develop (or up to 2 hours in the fridge if time allows).

Step two Heat a griddle or heavy-based frying pan until it is smoking hot. Place the chicken pieces skin-side down on to the hot pan and leave to cook for 4 minutes without moving, then carefully turn over; if the chicken is sticking, this means that it is not ready to be turned, so leave it for a minute or so longer.

Step three Once all the chicken has been turned, reduce the heat slightly and cook for a further 6–7 minutes or until the meat is tender and cooked through. Place the chicken onto serving plates and quickly grill the reserved orange wedges: this will only take a minute or so in a hot pan and the bar marks look great. Place around the chicken, garnish with the lime zest and serve with leafy salad or steamed rice and sweet chilli sauce.

Serves 4

2 tbsp olive oil

2 garlic cloves, thinly sliced

2 tbsp light muscovado sugar

1–2 tsp dried chilli flakes

8 large boneless, skin-on chicken thighs

1 large orange, cut into wedges

salt and freshly ground black pepper

to garnish

grated zest of 1 lime

to serve

lightly dressed leafy salad or steamed fragrant rice

sweet chilli sauce

Honey-glazed Duck with Sticky Rice

I love duck and this is one of my favourite ways of cooking it. The longer you can leave it to marinate the better – up to 24 hours in the fridge is best. Sushi rice is available in Asian stores and good supermarkets, but if you can't get hold of it use a fragrant rice such as Thai or basmati.

Serves 4

3 tbsp clear honey

3 tbsp dark soy sauce

juice and finely grated zest of 1 small orange

2 tbsp sesame seeds

4 x 175–200g (6–7oz) skin-on duck breasts

275g (10oz) sushi rice

120ml (4fl oz) chicken stock

salt

to garnish

fresh coriander leaves

shredded spring onions

Step one Preheat the oven to 200°C/400°F/gas 6. Place the honey in a shallow, non-metallic dish and add the soy sauce, orange juice and zest and sesame seeds, and mix well. Add the duck, turning to coat, and set aside at room temperature for 15 minutes (or longer in the fridge), turning occasionally.

Step two To make the sticky rice, rinse the rice thoroughly under cold running water and place in a pan with 600ml (1 pint) of cold water. Add a pinch of salt and bring to the boil, then stir once. Reduce the heat, cover and simmer for 8 minutes until all the water is completely absorbed. Turn off the heat and leave the rice to steam for at least 4–6 minutes until tender – it should sit happily for up to 20 minutes with the lid on.

Step three Heat a large, ovenproof frying pan until searing hot. Drain the marinade from the duck and reserve, then put the duck in the pan skin-side down and quickly seal, making sure the skin is slightly blackened. Turn over and just seal, then transfer to the oven and roast for 8–10 minutes until just tender but still slightly pink in the middle. If you prefer your duck more well done, give it another 2–3 minutes.

Step four Tip the reserved marinade into a small pan along with the stock and bring to the boil, then reduce the heat and simmer gently for 3–4 minutes until reduced, stirring occasionally. Meanwhile, remove the duck from the oven and leave to rest for 5 minutes in a warm place, then carve on the diagonal.

Step five Spoon the rice into warmed bowls, arrange the duck on top, drizzle around the reduced sauce and garnish with the coriander leaves and spring onions.

Oriental Turkey with Hot-wok Vegetables

Turkey meat is not only economical to buy but is also very lean and therefore low in fat. Here it is marinated and served in a quick oriental-style stir fry. If you fancy a change, why not try this recipe with chicken or pork escalopes. I've even made it with firm fish fillets.

Step one In a large shallow, non-metallic dish mix together the sherry, chilli sauce, soy sauce, sesame oil and ginger. Coat the turkey escalopes with the marinade. Cover and leave to marinate for at least 30 minutes, or overnight in the fridge if you have time.

Step two Preheat a large ridged griddle pan, or a frying pan, until smoking. Remove the turkey from the marinade, reserving the marinade, lay the meat in the pan and sear for 2–3 minutes on each side.

Step three Meanwhile, heat the sunflower oil in a large wok or frying pan and stir-fry the chilli and mushrooms for 2 minutes. Pour over the marinade and bring to the boil. Stir in the spring onions and pak choy and stir fry for 1–2 minutes until the vegetables are just wilted and the sauce has thickened. Serve immediately with the seared turkey escalopes.

Serves 4

2 tbsp dry sherry

1 tbsp sweet chilli sauce

2 tbsp dark soy sauce

1 tsp sesame oil

2.5cm (1in) piece fresh root ginger, peeled and shredded

4 x 150g (5oz) turkey escalopes

2 tsp sunflower oil

1 red chilli, seeded and thinly sliced

225g (8oz) shiitake mushrooms, halved

6 spring onions, trimmed and thinly sliced

4 large heads of pak choy, trimmed and separated into individual leaves

Chargrilled Chicken on Avocado Salad

This is a great main course salad. It requires a little bit of last-minute work but it's worth it, believe me.

Serves 6

450g (1lb) skinned mini chicken fillets

juice of ½ small lemon

6 tbsp olive oil

½ tsp salt

freshly ground black pepper

for the salad

175g (6oz) frozen peas

1 × 225g (8oz) bag baby leaf spinach

2 small ripe but firm avocados

salt and freshly ground black pepper

for the salad dressing

8 tbsp extra-virgin olive oil

2 tbsp red wine vinegar

a good pinch of caster sugar

2 shallots, halved and thinly sliced

2 tbsp mint leaves, chopped

to garnish

a small handful of mint leaves

Step one Put the chicken fillets into a shallow dish. Whisk together the lemon juice, oil, salt and some pepper, pour over the chicken and mix together. Set aside for at least 30 minutes. If using a charcoal barbecue, light it 30 minutes before you want to start cooking. If using a gas barbecue, light it 10 minutes beforehand. Alternatively, you can use a ridged griddle pan or frying pan.

Step two For the salad dressing, whisk together the oil, vinegar, sugar and some salt and pepper to taste in a bowl. Stir in the shallots and set aside.

Step three Drop the peas into a pan of boiling salted water, bring back to the boil and drain immediately. Refresh under cold water and drain well. Spread the spinach leaves over the base of 6 serving plates. Halve the avocados, remove the stones, then quarter the fruit and carefully peel. Cut across into slices and scatter on top of the spinach.

Step four Remove the chicken fillets from the marinade and season with a little salt. Grill or barbecue over a medium heat for 4–5 minutes on each side. Transfer to a plate, cool slightly, then arrange over the top of the salads. Stir the peas and chopped mint into the dressing, spoon over the chicken and salad and scatter with a few small mint leaves to garnish.

Cinnamon-scented Duck on Cherry Sauce

Call me old-fashioned if you like, but this is a classic and I want to see it back on our tables. You don't need to add any oil to the pan when frying the duck as the natural fat will be released as it cooks.

Step one Prick the skin on the duck breasts with a fork, then rub in the salt and cinnamon. Pour the port in a shallow dish, mix in the juice from the cherries and the thyme, and sit the duck skin-side up in the mixture so the flesh marinates while the skin takes in the salt and cinnamon. Set aside for 15 minutes or up to 1 hour.

Step two Remove the duck from the marinade, reserving the marinade, and pat the duck dry. Heat a large, non-stick frying pan and cook the duck, skin-side down, for 8–10 minutes until crisp and golden. Remove from the pan and drain off all the excess fat.

Step three Return the duck to the pan skin-side up. Pour the marinade mixture around the duck, bring to the boil and simmer for 12–15 minutes until the duck is cooked through but still a little pink in the centre. Remove the duck from the pan and rest on a plate for a few minutes.

Step four Check the seasoning and stir in the cherries and balsamic vinegar. Simmer for a minute or two until the cherries are warmed through. Then spoon the cherry sauce onto plates, place the breasts on top of the sauce and garnish with a sprig of fresh thyme, if liked.

Serves 4

4 x 225g (8oz) skin-on duck breasts

½ tsp sea salt

½ tsp ground cinnamon

100ml (4fl oz) ruby port

1 x 425g tin pitted black cherries in syrup

4 fresh sprigs of thyme, plus extra for garnish

½ tsp balsamic vinegar

Catalan Chicken Stew with Peppers, Olives and Smoked Paprika

Cooking a dish in one pot not only saves on the washing up, but all the lovely flavours mingle together and the aromas are heavenly.

Serves 4

2 tbsp olive oil

4 chicken thighs and 2 chicken breasts, cut into halves

2 red onions, sliced

1 red pepper, sliced

2 garlic cloves, crushed

250g (9oz) chorizo sausage, diced

1 x 400g (14oz) tin chopped tomatoes

250ml (8fl oz) chicken stock

150ml (¼ pint) dry white wine

1 rounded tsp smoked paprika

a pinch of saffron

50g (2oz) raisins

2 strips orange zest

1 sprig fresh thyme

about 20 olives

1 x 400g (14oz) tin chickpeas, rinsed

2 tbsp chopped fresh parsley

salt and freshly ground black pepper

to serve

rice

Step one Preheat the oven to 170°C/325°F/gas 3. In a large frying pan heat 1 tablespoon of the oil. Add the chicken and brown really well all over. Transfer to a casserole dish.

Step two Use the remaining oil to cook the onions in the frying pan until they turn golden at the edges. Add the pepper and garlic and cook for a further minute. Remove from the pan with a slotted spoon and add to the chicken. Brown the chorizo in the frying pan and add this to the chicken.

Step three Pour the tomatoes, stock and wine over the chicken, and add the smoked paprika and saffron (if using). Add the raisins (if using), orange zest and thyme, season and mix well. Add the olives and chickpeas, bring to the boil, then cover and transfer to the oven for about 40 minutes. Scatter with the parsley and serve with rice.

I like to serve rice with this dish, especially Camargue red rice, which you can buy from smart delis.

Thai-style Chicken, Corn and Prawn Cakes with Sweet Chilli Sauce

As my wife says, these are simply delicious and so easy to prepare. The curry paste quantity is approximate, depending on how spicy you like your food: 1 tablespoon = mild; 3 tablespoons = hot.

Step one Roughly chop the chicken breasts and place in the bowl of a food-processor. Add the prawns, egg white, garlic and curry paste. Process until finely chopped. Tip into a bowl, add the breadcrumbs, sweetcorn, coriander and spring onions, and mix until well combined. Using wet hands, shape the mixture into approximately 16 small patties.

Step two To make the sweet chilli sauce, mix the three sauces together, add the cucumber (if using) and set aside.

Step three Heat the oil in a large frying pan. Cook the patties in batches, for about 1–2 minutes on each side, until golden brown. Drain on kitchen paper and serve with lime wedges and the sweet chilli sauce.

If you're using a food-processor, make the breadcrumbs in it before you blitz the chicken – it saves on the washing-up.

Serves 4

2 skinless chicken breasts

250g (9oz) raw tiger prawns, peeled and deveined

1 egg white

1 garlic clove, crushed

1–3 tbsp Thai red curry paste

50g (2oz) fresh breadcrumbs

1 x 195g (7oz) tin sweetcorn, drained

2 tbsp chopped fresh coriander

4 spring onions, sliced

2 tbsp sunflower oil

for the sweet chilli sauce

4 tbsp sweet chilli sauce

1 tsp soy sauce

1 tsp Thai fish sauce

5cm (2in) piece cucumber, peeled, seeded and finely chopped (optional)

to serve

lime wedges

For more recipes from My Kitchen Table, sign up for our newsletter at www.mykitchentable.co.uk/newsletter

American-style Seared Chicken Salad

This is a variation on the famous Caesar salad but is much easier to prepare. If time allows, rub the paprika mixture into the chicken, cover with clingfilm and chill overnight to allow the flavours to penetrate the flesh.

Serves 2

3 tbsp mayonnaise

1 tbsp crème fraîche

2 garlic cloves, crushed

1 tsp Dijon mustard

1 tsp Worcestershire sauce

¼ tsp Tabasco sauce

2 anchovy fillets, crushed to a paste

4 tbsp olive oil

1 tsp sweet paprika

2 tbsp chopped fresh flat-leaf parsley

2 chicken breast fillets

2 slices country-style bread, crusts removed and cut into cubes

1 large cos lettuce

40g (1½ oz) freshly grated Parmesan

salt and freshly ground black pepper

Step one Place the mayonnaise in a small bowl and mix in the crème fraîche. Add half the garlic, the mustard, Worcestershire sauce, Tabasco sauce and anchovies, then beat until well combined. Season to taste. Cover with clingfilm and chill until ready to use.

Step two Heat a griddle pan until searing hot. Place half the olive oil in a shallow, non-metallic dish and mix with the remaining garlic plus the paprika, parsley and a teaspoon each of salt and pepper. Slash the chicken fillets and rub the oil mixture into the flesh, then place in the griddle pan and cook for 10–12 minutes, turning once, until cooked through and completely tender. Transfer to a plate and leave to rest for a minute or two.

Step three Meanwhile, make some croûtons. Heat a frying pan. Toss the bread cubes in a bowl with the remaining oil and season generously. Add to the heated pan and sauté for 6–8 minutes until evenly golden.

Step four Break the large outer lettuce leaves roughly, keeping the smaller leaves whole. Toss with the mayonnaise mixture and two-thirds of the grated Parmesan. Arrange the leaves in the centre of 2 plates, scatter with the croûtons, then garnish with the remaining Parmesan. Carve each chicken breast on the diagonal and arrange on the salads to serve.

Calypso Pepperpot Chicken with Plantain

This is equally great cooked on a barbie or on a griddle pan. You can marinate the chicken overnight; just cover with clingfilm and refrigerate. Plantains belong to the banana family. They are ready to use when the skins begin to go black, like an over-ripe banana.

Step one Preheat the grill to medium. Place 2 teaspoons of the pepper sauce in a shallow non-metallic dish and mix in the garlic, paprika, thyme, half the coriander, and half a teaspoon of salt and 2 teaspoons of cracked black pepper. Add the oil and stir until well combined. Lightly slash each chicken breast and coat well with the pepper mixture.

Step two Grill the chicken for 6–8 minutes on each side until cooked through and lightly charred.

Step three Place the coconut cream and mango pieces in a pan and bring to the boil, then reduce the heat and simmer gently for about 5 minutes or until the mango is tender. Add the remaining teaspoon of pepper sauce, the remaining coriander and the lime juice. Blend to a purée in a food-processor or with a hand blender. Season to taste with pepper and transfer to a bowl.

Step four Peel the plantains and cut each one across into two pieces, then cut each piece in half, lengthways. Heat a large frying pan and melt the butter, add the plantain pieces and fry over a medium-high heat for about 2 minutes on each side until lightly golden. Drain on kitchen paper. To serve, arrange the plantain pieces on plates with the calypso chicken. Divide the coconut sauce between individual dishes and place on the side of each plate. Serve at once.

Serves 4

3 tsp West Indian hot pepper sauce

2 garlic cloves, crushed

1 tsp paprika

1 tsp dried thyme

2 tbsp chopped fresh coriander, plus sprigs for the garnish

3 tbsp olive oil

4 boneless, skinless chicken breasts

200ml (7fl oz) coconut cream

1 small ripe mango, peeled, stoned and diced (about 175g/6oz in total)

juice of ½ lime

2 large ripe plantains

40g (1½ oz) unsalted butter

salt and cracked black pepper

Tempting Turkey, Leek and Mushroom Pies

These pies are fab served with garlic mash. You could also use chicken instead of turkey, and, if you like a bit of kick to your food, try adding 1 teaspoon of cayenne pepper to the flour.

Serves 4

2 tbsp plain flour, plus extra for dusting

500g (1lb 2oz) turkey breast steaks, trimmed and cut into bite-sized pieces

4 tbsp olive oil

2 leeks, white part only, sliced

150g (5oz) chestnut mushrooms, sliced

2 garlic cloves, crushed

120ml (4fl oz) dry white wine

150ml (¼ pint) chicken stock (see tip)

120ml (4fl oz) double cream

2–3 tbsp chopped fresh flat-leaf parsley

150g (5oz) ready-rolled puff pastry, thawed if frozen

1 egg yolk mixed with 1 tbsp water

salt and freshly ground black pepper

Step one Preheat the oven to 220°C/425°F/gas 7. Place the flour in a large bowl and season generously, then use to coat the turkey pieces, shaking off any excess. Heat 2 tbsp of the oil in a large, heavy-based pan, add the turkey pieces and cook for a minute or two on each side until beginning to brown. Remove from the pan and set aside.

Step two Add the remaining oil to the pan, then stir in the leeks, mushrooms and garlic and cook over a medium heat for 3 minutes until softened but not coloured. Return the turkey to the pan, then pour in the wine, bring to the boil and cook for 1–2 minutes, scraping the bottom of the pan with a wooden spoon to remove any sediment.

Step three Pour the stock into the pan, along with the cream, and simmer for 6 minutes until slightly reduced and thickened, stirring occasionally. Stir in the parsley and season to taste. Ladle the mixture into 4 x 300ml (½ pint) individual pie dishes; allow to cool slightly so that a light skin forms on top.

Step four Meanwhile, on a lightly floured work surface roll out the pastry to about 5mm (¼ in) thick and cut out 4 lids large enough to fit the tops of your pies. Brush the lips of the pie dishes with the egg wash and stick down the pastry lids. Brush each lid with egg wash and gently press down along the sides to seal, then cut a small slit in each pie lid. Bake for about 25 minutes or until the pies are golden brown. Serve immediately.

If you can't buy fresh chicken stock, use half a chicken stock cube dissolved in 150ml (¼ pint) boiling water.

Yakitori Chicken Skewers

These skewers are incredibly easy to make but taste so delicious they'll be gone before you know it. Traditional Japanese ingredients are now becoming much more widely available so look out for them in your local supermarket.

Step one Put the soy sauce, mirin, sake and sugar into a small pan. Bring to the boil, then reduce the heat and simmer for about 5 minutes, stirring occasionally, until the mixture has reduced and become slightly syrupy. Place in a shallow non-metallic dish and leave to cool.

Step two Cut the chicken thighs into 2cm (¾in) pieces and add to the cooled marinade. Cover with clingfilm and chill for at least 2 hours, or overnight if time allows.

Step three Light the barbecue. Soak 8 x 15cm (6in) wooden skewers in a shallow dish of cold water for 30 minutes to prevent them from burning on the barbecue.

Step four Thread the chicken onto skewers and barbecue for 6–8 minutes on medium hot coals, turning and basting with the marinade now and then. Arrange onto warmed plates to serve, with small bowls of soy sauce on the side for dipping.

Serves 4

6 tbsp Japanese soy sauce, plus extra for dipping

3 tbsp mirin

2 tbsp sake

1 tbsp caster sugar

450g (1lb) boneless, skinless chicken thighs

Monzarelli's Mediterranean Burgers

This dish has all my favourite Mediterranean flavours in it: pine nuts, basil, sun-dried tomatoes, garlic and Parmesan – delicious.

Serves 4

500g (1lb 2oz) good-quality sausage meat

8 sun-dried tomatoes in oil, very finely chopped

2 garlic cloves, finely chopped

2 tbsp freshly grated Parmesan

2 tbsp toasted pine nuts, roughly chopped

2 tbsp shredded fresh basil

2 tbsp chopped fresh parsley

salt and freshly ground black pepper

to serve

Italian bread

Step one Heat the grill or light the barbecue. Place the sausage meat in a large bowl and stir in the sun-dried tomatoes, garlic, Parmesan, pine nuts, basil, parsley and plenty of seasoning.

Step two Using damp hands, shape the mixture into 4 even-sized burgers. Cook under a medium grill or over medium coals for 5–6 minutes on each side until well browned and completely cooked through. Serve with nice Italian bread such as ciabatta, and hearty red wine.

Creamy Spaghetti Carbonara

For a change, you could replace the bacon in this recipe with strips of smoked salmon, which obviously don't need any cooking, and use dill instead of parsley.

Step one Plunge the spaghetti in a large pan of boiling, salted water, stir and cook at a rolling boil for 10–12 minutes until al dente.

Step two Meanwhile, heat the oil in a frying pan. Add the shallot and garlic and sauté for 2–3 minutes until softened but not coloured. Stir in the pancetta and cook for another 2–3 minutes until sizzling and lightly golden.

Step three Break the egg into a bowl. Add the cream, two-thirds of the Parmesan and all the parsley. Add some seasoning, then whisk lightly.

Step four Drain the spaghetti and return to the hot pan. Quickly pour in the egg mixture and the pancetta mixture and toss well to combine; the heat from the spaghetti will cook the egg. Serve with the remaining Parmesan scattered on top.

Serves 2

175–225g (6–8oz) spaghetti

1 tbsp olive oil

1 shallot, finely chopped

1 small garlic clove, finely chopped

100g (4oz) pancetta or streaky bacon lardons

1 egg

3 tbsp double cream

50g (2oz) freshly grated Parmesan

½ tbsp flat-leaf parsley leaves, chopped

salt and freshly ground black pepper

Szechuan Peppered Steak with Spiced Redcurrants

Szechuan peppercorns are more aromatic than peppercorns. They are not related to peppercorns, but are the dried berries of an oriental shrub called the prickly ash tree.

Serves 4

1 tbsp Szechuan peppercorns

1 tbsp black peppercorns

4 x 150g (5oz) rump steaks, well trimmed

1 tbsp sunflower oil

75g (3oz) caster sugar

a pinch of dried chilli flakes

1 cinnamon stick, crushed into tiny pieces, or 1 tsp ground cinnamon

200g (7oz) redcurrants, removed from stalks (see tip)

50g (2oz) unsalted butter

salt

to serve

sautéd new potatoes (optional)

Step one Using a pestle and mortar, grind the Szechuan and black peppercorns to a fine powder, (a bit of texture is good). Rub each of the steaks with a little oil to help the peppercorns stick, and press the peppercorn mixture on to each steak, making sure they are evenly coated. Set on a large plate, cover loosely with clingfilm, then set aside at room temperature.

Step two Place the sugar in a small, heavy-based pan with 2 tablespoons of water. Cook the mixture over a gentle heat for a couple of minutes, stirring until the sugar has completely dissolved. Increase the heat, bring to the boil and add the chilli and cinnamon, then boil fast for 1 minute. Add the redcurrants, bring to a gentle simmer and cook for 4–5 minutes or until the currants are starting to soften but are still holding their shape. Remove from the heat and allow to stand for a few minutes so that the flavours can combine.

Step three Melt the butter in a large, non-stick frying pan. When the butter is starting to foam, add the steaks and cook on one side for 2 minutes, then turn, reduce the heat slightly and cook for a further 3 minutes for rare. If you prefer your steaks medium, increase the cooking time by 1 minute for each side; for well done, increase by 2 minutes for each side.

Step four Transfer the steaks to warmed plates and season with salt to taste. Leave to rest for a few minutes, then add a dollop of spiced redcurrants to each plate, with some sautéd potatoes.

The best way to remove redcurrants from their stems is to use a fork; hold the end of the stem and push through the prongs, dragging the fork downwards.

Smouldering Smoked Chinese Roast Ribs

Try this delicious marinade with any type of pork on the bone – the shoulder blade is particularly good.

Serves 4

2 garlic cloves, crushed

½ tsp salt

4 tbsp caster sugar

1 tbsp Hoisin sauce

1 tbsp yellow bean or barbecue sauce

2 tbsp soy sauce

1 tbsp Shaoxing rice wine or dry sherry

a few drops of red food colouring

1 sheet pork ribs (about 675 g/1½ lb)

Step one Mix together the garlic, salt, sugar, Hoisin sauce, soy sauce, yellow bean sauce, rice wine and food colouring to make a marinade.

Step two Place the ribs in a roasting tin and pour the marinade over. Refrigerate for up to an hour, basting occasionally with the mixture.

Step three Cook over medium coals or under a preheated grill for about 40 minutes, turning occasionally and brushing with any remaining marinade, until cooked through. Carve between the ribs and serve.

Lightning Lamb Dhansak

Lamb dhansak is one of the most popular dishes on any Indian menu and absolutely delicious. For complete authenticity, it can take a whole day to make the dish, but this lightning version combines all the flavours and tastes superb. Tamarind paste is available in large supermarkets or good delis.

Serves 4

500g (1lb 2oz) cubed lamb

2 tbsp garam masala

2–3 tbsp vegetable oil

2 onions, thinly sliced

2 garlic cloves, thinly sliced

200g (7oz) diced pumpkin or squash

100g (4oz) dried red lentils

600ml (1 pint) hot vegetable stock

1 tbsp curry paste

1 tbsp tamarind paste

25g (1oz) caster sugar

2 tbsp chopped fresh mint or coriander

juice of 1 lemon

salt and freshly ground black pepper

to serve

Pilau rice

Step one Toss the lamb in the garam masala. Heat 1 tablespoon of the oil in a large pan and brown the lamb briefly. Transfer to a plate and set aside.

Step two Add a little more oil to the pan, then add the onions, garlic and pumpkin or squash and cook for 5 minutes until softened and beginning to brown.

Step three Now add the lentils, stock, curry paste, tamarind paste and sugar and stir the lamb back into the pan. Bring to the boil, cover, reduce the heat and simmer for 25–30 minutes, stirring occasionally, until the mixture is thickened and the ingredients are lovely and tender. Check the seasoning, then stir in the mint or coriander and lemon juice, to taste. Serve with pilau rice.

Beef Kofta Kebabs with Mango and Mint Raita

You can make these kebabs with minced lamb instead of beef if you prefer, and they are great cooked on the barbecue, too. Just remember, don't use extra-lean mince for them: the fattiness of ordinary mince will help keep them nice and moist during cooking.

Step one Soak 12 wooden skewers in cold water for about 20 minutes. Put the onion into a food-processor and blend until very finely chopped. Tip into a bowl and add the rest of the ingredients, apart from the oil. Add about half a teaspoon of salt and some cayenne pepper and mix together thoroughly with your hands.

Step two Divide the mixture into 12 equally sized pieces, then shape roughly into sausages. Push a soaked skewer up through the length of each sausage and squash the meat more firmly onto the sticks.

Step three For the raita, peel the mango, then slice the flesh away from the stone. Cut it into small pieces and mix with the rest of the ingredients and a little salt to taste.

Step four Heat a ridged or heavy-based frying pan over a high heat until smoking hot. Reduce the heat to medium-high, brush the kebabs with a little oil and cook for 4–5 minutes, turning now and again until nicely browned and cooked through. Serve with the mango and mint raita.

Serves 4

1 small onion, cut into chunks

750g (1½ lb) minced beef

1 tbsp ground coriander

1 tbsp ground cumin

¼ tsp ground turmeric

1 tsp garam masala

2 garlic cloves, crushed

2.5cm (1in) fresh root ginger, peeled and grated

2 tbsp whole-milk natural yoghurt

a little sunflower oil, for brushing

salt and cayenne pepper

for the raita

1 small, ripe but firm mango

175g (6oz) whole-milk natural yoghurt

1 tbsp sieved mango chutney

2 tbsp chopped fresh mint

Seared Sirloin Steak with Blue Cheese Butter and Shoestring Chips

The recipe for the blue cheese butter will make slightly more than you need for this dish. The extra will keep in the freezer, tightly wrapped in clingfilm, and can be used with chicken or on baked potatoes.

Serves 2

2 x 175g (6oz) sirloin steaks, each cut 2.5cm (1in) thick

vegetable oil, for brushing

salt and freshly ground black pepper

for the chips

450g (1lb) floury potatoes, such as Maris Piper

sunflower oil, for deep-frying

for the blue cheese butter

25g (1oz) slightly salted butter, at room temperature

15g (½oz) full-fat cream cheese

1 tsp wholegrain mustard

25g (1oz) blue cheese, such as Roquefort or Stilton

the leaves from 3 sprigs curly parsley, chopped

to serve

tomato and red onion salad

Step one For the blue cheese butter, place the butter, cream cheese and mustard into a small bowl and mix together well. Crumble in the blue cheese, add the parsley and mix with the back of a fork into a coarse paste. Set aside (or in the fridge if it's a warm day).

Step two To prepare the chips, peel the potatoes and cut them lengthways into slices about 5mm (¼in) thick. Then cut them once more into long, thin chips. Heat some oil for deep-frying to 190°C/375°F.

Step three Deep-fry the chips, in two batches, for 2–3 minutes until soft but not browned. Lift out and drain briefly on kitchen paper. Bring the oil back up to temperature.

Step four Brush the steaks on both sides with a little oil and season well with salt and pepper. Heat a ridged cast-iron griddle or a heavy-based frying pan over a high heat until smoking hot. Add the steaks and cook for 1½ minutes on each side for rare, 2 minutes for medium-rare, pressing down on top of them with a fish slice as they cook.

Step five While the steaks are cooking on the second side, drop the chips back into the oil and fry for a further 1–2 minutes until crisp and golden. Drain well on lots of kitchen paper and sprinkle with salt. Transfer the steaks to warmed plates and spoon some of the blue cheese butter on top. Pile some of the chips alongside and serve with a simple salad of tomatoes and red onion.

Shepherd's Pie with Irish Champ Mash Topping

Using lamb gravy in the filling gives this pie a lovely flavour. Just remember to save some next time you do a roast.

Step one Heat the oil in a large pan, add the onion and cook over a medium heat for 5 minutes until soft and lightly browned. Add the carrots and cook for a further 2 minutes. Add the minced lamb, increase the heat to high, and cook for 3–4 minutes, breaking up the meat with a wooden spoon as it browns.

Step two Add the thyme leaves, Worcestershire sauce, tomato purée and gravy or stock to the pan and simmer for about 20 minutes until the liquid has reduced and the mixture has thickened slightly. Season to taste, then spoon into a shallow, 2.4 litre (4 pint) ovenproof dish.

Step three Meanwhile, preheat the oven to 200°C/400°F/gas 6 and make the champ mash. Put the potatoes into a pan of cold salted water, bring to the boil and simmer for 20 minutes until tender. Drain well and mash until smooth.

Step four Melt the butter in another pan, add the spring onions and cook gently for 2 minutes until soft. Stir into the mashed potato, along with the milk and some seasoning. Spoon the champ mash over the top of the lamb, spread out evenly and then rough up a little with a fork. Bake for 30–35 minutes until bubbling hot and golden brown.

Serves 4

2 tbsp sunflower oil

1 medium onion, finely chopped

225g (8oz) peeled carrots, finely diced

900g (2lb) lean minced lamb

2 tsp thyme leaves

1 tbsp Worcestershire sauce

1 tsp tomato purée

300ml (10fl oz) lamb gravy or meat stock

salt and freshly ground black pepper

for the Irish champ mash

1.25kg (2½ lb) peeled floury potatoes, such as Maris Piper, cut into chunks

50g (2oz) butter

2 bunches spring onions, sliced

3–4 tbsp milk

Sirloin Skewers with Sweet Peppers and Shiitake Mushrooms

This dish is full of fresh, clean flavours; the sauce created is similar to teriyaki but not quite as sweet. Shiitake mushrooms are excellent in all manner of Oriental dishes as they have a pronounced mushroomy scent and flavour.

Serves 4

2 tsp sesame oil

4 tbsp dark soy sauce

6 tbsp sake or dry white wine

1 tbsp freshly grated root ginger

2 garlic cloves, finely chopped

550g (1¼ lb) sirloin steak, cut into 2.5cm (1in) cubes

1 tbsp sunflower oil

2 large red peppers, seeded and cut into 4cm (1½ in) slices

120g (4½ oz) shiitake mushrooms, halved

1 bunch spring onions, cut into 4cm (1½ in) lengths

salt and freshly ground black pepper

to serve

fragrant jasmine rice

Step one In a shallow, non-metallic dish place the sesame oil, soy sauce, sake or wine, ginger and garlic, and mix well. Season to taste and stir in the steak cubes to coat them well, then set aside to marinate for 10 minutes at room temperature (or cover with clingfilm and chill for up to 24 hours).

Step two Heat a large, non-stick frying pan. Drain the steak from the marinade, reserving it to use later, then thread the steak onto 8 x 15cm (6in) wooden skewers. When the pan is smoking hot, add the skewers and sear on all sides – you may have to do this in two batches, depending on the size of your pan. Transfer to a warmed plate and keep warm.

Step three Add the sunflower oil to the same pan, and then tip in the peppers and mushrooms. Sauté for 2 minutes, then add the spring onions and sauté for a further minute. Add the reserved marinade, reduce the heat and continue to cook for about 1 minute or until the vegetables are just tender and the sauce has slightly thickened, stirring occasionally.

Step four Check the seasoning and add more if necesssary. Arrange the vegetables on warmed plates, add the skewers on top and spoon over any remaining sauce. Serve with fragrant jasmine rice.

For a video masterclass on marinating, go to
www.mykitchentable.co.uk/videos/marinatingmeat

Gremolata Lamb Cutlets with Roasted New Potatoes, Courgettes and Tomatoes

A blend of garlic, lemon zest, flat-leaf parsley and quality breadcrumbs gives you gremolata – the perfect topping for all sorts of meats, fish and vegetables. Try to use loin lamb cutlets, as they usually have less fat, or buy a rack of lamb and slice it into cutlets.

Step one Preheat the oven to 220°C/425°F/gas 7.

Step two Wash and thickly slice the potatoes. Place in a roasting tin and drizzle with 2 tbsp of the oil. Season and add the thyme, then roast for about 30 minutes, or until the potatoes start to turn golden brown.

Step three Slice the courgettes, add to the roasting tin along with the tomatoes, and continue to cook for a further 15 minutes. Meanwhile, mix all the gremolata ingredients together, season and mix well. Press the mixture all over the lamb cutlets.

Step four Heat the remaining oil in a large frying pan, add half the cutlets and lightly brown on both sides; take care when turning them not to knock off the crust. Transfer to the roasting tin, placing the cutlets on top of the potatoes. Brown the remaining cutlets and add to the potatoes. Return to the oven for a further 10 minutes. Remove the thyme and serve with freshly steamed broccoli.

Serves 4

500g (1 lb 2oz) new potatoes

3 tbsp olive oil

1 large sprig fresh thyme

2 medium courgettes

225g (8oz) cherry tomatoes

8–12 lamb cutlets

salt and freshly ground black pepper

for the gremolata

50g (2oz) fresh white breadcrumbs

2 tbsp freshly grated Parmesan

grated zest of 1 lemon

2 garlic cloves, crushed

3 tbsp chopped fresh flat-leaf parsley

2 tbsp olive oil

to serve

steamed broccoli

Southern-style Sausage Jambalaya

This tasty Cajun dish is perfect fork-food for dinner in front of the telly.

Serves 4

2 tbsp sunflower oil

100g (4oz) chorizo
thickly sliced

1 x 225g (8oz) smoked
pork sausage ring,
thickly sliced

4 garlic cloves,
crushed

1 medium onion,
chopped

1 red pepper, cut into
chunky strips

1 green pepper, cut
into chunky strips

2 celery sticks, sliced

1 tsp chilli powder

1 tsp hot paprika

225g (8oz)
long-grain rice

1 tsp fresh thyme

2 bay leaves

400ml (14fl oz) passata

300ml (10fl oz)
chicken stock

225g (8oz) large
cooked, peeled
prawns

2 tbsp fresh parsley,
chopped

4 spring onions,
thinly sliced

salt and cayenne
pepper

Step one Heat the sunflower oil in a large, deep frying pan. Fry the chorizo and smoked pork sausage slices on both sides until golden. Lift out and set aside.

Step two Add the garlic to the pan, along with the onion, red and green peppers and celery, and fry for 5 minutes until they are all lightly browned. Add the chilli powder and paprika and cook for 1 minute. Stir in the browned sausages, the rice, thyme, bay leaves, passata, chicken stock, a good sprinkling of salt and some cayenne pepper. Bring to the boil, cover and reduce the heat, and simmer gently for 20 minutes.

Step three Tip the prawns into the pan, replace the cover and cook for a further 4–5 minutes. Uncover and fork the prawns and the parsley into the rice. Scatter over the spring onions and serve immediately.

Corned Beef Hash with Poached Egg

Originally from the southern states of the USA, this terrific comfort food can also be served with a fried egg and a good dollop of tomato ketchup on the side.

Step one Place the potatoes in a pan and cover with boiling water. Add a pinch of salt and bring to the boil, then cover and simmer for 5 minutes.

Step two Meanwhile, heat the oil in a large, heavy-based, non-stick frying pan. Add the onion and sauté for 3–4 minutes until softened. Drain the potatoes, then add the butter to the onion mixture. Once it is foaming, tip in the potatoes, season and sauté for 8–10 minutes until the potatoes are crisp and golden.

Step three To poach the eggs, heat 4cm (1½in) water in a large, deep frying pan until little bubbles begin to appear on the surface. Add 1 tablespoon white wine vinegar and ½ teaspoon salt. Break a very fresh egg into a teacup, then slide it gently into the water. Cook for 3½ minutes, making sure the water stays at a very gentle simmer. Life them out of the water with a slotted spoon and drain briefly on kitchen paper.

Step four Meanwhile, add the corned beef to the potato and onion mixture and continue to sauté for a further 3–4 minutes until the corned beef has broken down and crisped up in places. Stir in the parsley and season to taste. Serve on warmed plates with a poached egg on top.

Serves 2

550g (1¼lb) potatoes, cut into 1cm (½in) cubes

2 tbsp olive oil

1 large onion, chopped

knob of butter

1 x 200g (7oz) tin corned beef, cut into 1cm (½in) cubes

2 tbsp chopped fresh parsley

salt and freshly ground black pepper

for the poached eggs

1 tbsp white wine vinegar

½ tsp salt

2 eggs

to serve

tomato ketchup

Mexican Beef Fajitas

This is great for a Friday night supper. You can just put everything into the centre of the table and let everyone help themselves.

Serves 4

450g (1lb) rump, sirloin or fillet steak

1 red pepper

1 green pepper

1 small yellow pepper

2 large onions

150ml (¼ pint) soured cream

1 cos lettuce heart, finely shredded

3 tbsp sunflower oil

8–12 soft flour tortillas

salt and cayenne pepper

for the spicy tomato salsa

1 medium-hot green chilli, deseeded and finely chopped

1 small red onion, very finely chopped

1 ×200g (7oz) tin chopped tomatoes

juice of 1 lime

1 tbsp chopped fresh coriander

Step one Cut the steak into long thin strips. Season well with salt and some cayenne pepper and set to one side. Deseed and thickly slice the red, green and yellow peppers. Peel and thickly slice the onions. Preheat the grill to high.

Step two Mix the salsa ingredients together with a little salt to taste. Transfer to a serving bowl. Spoon the soured cream into another bowl and the shredded lettuce into a small salad bowl.

Step three Heat half the oil in a large frying pan. Add the onions, peppers and some seasoning and stir fry over a high heat for 5 minutes until soft and slightly browned. Tip onto a plate and set aside.

Step four Add half the remaining oil to the pan and, when really hot, add half the steak and stir fry for 3–4 minutes until well browned. Set aside with the peppers while you cook the remainder.

Step five Return everything to the pan and toss together briefly over a high heat. Warm the tortillas under the grill for 10 seconds. Wrap in a napkin and take to the table with the pan of steak and peppers and the bowls of salsa, lettuce and soured cream.

Step six To serve, lay a tortilla on a plate and spoon some of the beef and peppers down the centre. Spoon a little spicy tomato salsa and soured cream on top, sprinkle with lettuce, then roll up tightly and eat with your hands.

Roasted Onion, Rocket and Pecorino Salad

Roasted onions are absolutely delicious – I like to serve them hot as a side vegetable, but they also make an extra-special salad when tossed with peppery rocket and salty Parmesan or pecorino cheese.

Step one Preheat the oven to 190°C/375°F/gas 5.

Step two Place the onions in a shallow roasting tin and drizzle all over with the oil. Season generously and roast for 25–30 minutes until the onions are softened and nicely browned.

Step three Remove the onions from the oven and drizzle over the balsamic vinegar. Allow the onions to cool to room temperature. Using a swivel-style peeler, shave the cheese into wafer-thin slices. Arrange the rocket, roast onions and cheese on serving plates; drizzle with the pan juices and serve immediately.

Serves 4

12 button onions, halved

3 tbsp olive oil

sea salt and coarsely ground black pepper

1 tbsp balsamic vinegar

50g (2oz) Parmesan or Pecorino

100g (4oz) rocket leaves

Sweet Eddie Cajun Wedges

Whenever we are having a party I make trays of these wedges. They're always a winner and, dare I say it, cheap as chips. I normally cook them in advance and then just reheat them as they're needed. It's worth splashing out on a good-quality Cajun seasoning – look out for the ones sold in small foil packets, which are incredibly pungent.

Serves 4–6

4 x 175g (6oz) potatoes

4 x 175g (6oz) orange-fleshed sweet potatoes

4 tbsp olive oil

1–2 tbsp Cajun seasoning

for the dip

125g (4½ oz) cream cheese

150ml (¼ pint) soured cream

8 sun-blushed tomatoes, chopped

4 tbsp snipped fresh chives

salt and freshly ground black pepper

Step one Preheat the oven to 200°C/400°F/gas 6. Scrub the potatoes and sweet potatoes and cut each one into 6 evenly sized wedges. Place the potatoes in a pan of boiling water, return to the boil and blanch for 2–3 minutes, then quickly drain.

Step two Put the olive oil in a large roasting tin, then sprinkle in a teaspoon of salt and the Cajun seasoning to taste. Add the wedges and toss until they are all well coated in the flavoured oil, then arrange them in rows 'sitting' upright on their skins. Bake for 35–40 minutes until tender and lightly golden, with an extra 10–15 minutes if you like them really crunchy.

Step three To make the dip, place the cream cheese, soured cream and sun-blushed tomatoes in a food-processor or liquidizer and blitz to combine. Transfer to a serving bowl, stir in the chives and season to taste. Cover with clingfilm and chill until ready to use – the longer the better to allow the flavours to mingle.

Step four Pile the wedges onto a large, warmed serving platter and serve with the sun-blushed tomato and soured cream dip. Alternatively, allow them to cool and chill for up to 24 hours covered with clingfilm, then reheat in the oven for 15–20 minutes until piping hot.

Buttered Savoy Cabbage with Caraway

If you think you don't like cabbage, try this recipe, and you will be pleasantly surprised. It's just fantastic with Savoy cabbage but any green cabbage works really well with this technique. If you're feeling fiery, throw in a few chilli flakes when frying the caraway. It takes less than 5 minutes to cook, so start to prepare it just before you are ready to serve.

Step one Melt half the butter in a large heavy-based pan with a lid. Add the caraway seeds and stir-fry for 30 seconds or so until fragrant. Add 2 tablespoons of water and bring to the boil over a high heat.

Step two When the emulsion is boiling, add the cabbage all in one go with a pinch of salt, then cover the pan, shake vigorously and cook over a high heat for 1½ minutes. Give the pan another shake, cook for a further 1½ minutes, then remove from the heat. Season with pepper, then tip into a warmed bowl and serve at once, with the rest of the butter melting on top.

Serves 4–6

50g (2oz) butter

a pinch of caraway seeds

1 Savoy cabbage, trimmed, core removed, and shredded

salt and freshly ground black pepper

Vegetable Creole Crunch Salad

The perfect alternative to coleslaw, with more colour and flavour –
and it's healthier too. Can the crunch get any better? Serve it up as an
accompaniment to grilled meat or fish, or spoon into a fluffy baked jacket
potato – ideal for a quick healthy supper.

Serves 6

275g (10oz) white
cabbage, cored and
very thinly shredded

2 celery sticks,
thinly sliced

1 green pepper,
seeded and very
thinly sliced

4 spring onions,
trimmed and
thinly sliced

2 tbsp chopped
fresh dill (optional)

1 tsp caraway seeds
(optional)

a pinch of cayenne
pepper

for the dressing

½ tbsp Dijon mustard

1 tsp creamed
horseradish

1 tsp Tabasco sauce

1 tbsp red wine
vinegar

1 tbsp olive oil

2 tbsp Greek yoghurt

salt and freshly ground
black pepper

Step one In a large bowl mix together the cabbage, celery,
green pepper and spring onions.

Step two To make the dressing, in a small bowl mix together
the mustard, creamed horseradish, Tabasco sauce and vinegar.
Gradually whisk in the oil. Stir in the yoghurt and season well.

Step three Stir the dressing, and the chopped dill and caraway
seeds, if using, into the vegetables just before serving so that
the cabbage stays nice and crunchy. Dust all over with cayenne
pepper and serve.

For a video masterclass on chopping veg, go to
www.mykitchentable.co.uk/videos/choppingvegetables

Puy Lentil, Red Onion and Sun-dried Tomato Salad

Make this salad a little while before you need it so that all the flavours have time to soak into the lentils. Greeny, slate-grey Puy lentils definitely have the best flavour of the dark lentils. If your local supermarket doesn't have any, you should have more luck in a health food shop. Or, if all else fails and you're in a hurry, use tinned green lentils, which require no cooking.

Step one Put the lentils into a pan with the bay leaf, vinegar, 1 garlic clove, sugar and a little salt and pepper. Cover with 1.2 litres (2 pints) of cold water, bring to the boil, then reduce the heat and leave to simmer for about 25 minutes until just tender but still holding their shape.

Step two Drain the lentils well. Discard the bay leaf and garlic clove. Tip the lentils into a salad bowl and leave to go cold.

Step three Finely chop the remaining garlic clove and stir it into the lentils, along with all the remaining ingredients. Season to taste with salt and pepper and chill in the fridge for up to 2 hours before serving.

Serves 8

225g (8oz) dried Puy lentils, picked over for stones

1 fresh bay leaf

1 tsp red wine vinegar

2 garlic cloves, peeled and left whole

pinch of caster sugar

1 large red onion, finely chopped

50g (2oz) sun-dried tomatoes in oil, drained and chopped

1–2 tbsp balsamic vinegar

4 tbsp extra-virgin olive oil

100g (4oz) goats' cheese or feta cheese, crumbled

3 tbsp chopped fresh flat-leaf parsley

salt and freshly ground black pepper

Roasted Butternut Squash and Root Vegetables

These roasted veggies are delicious served either hot or at room temperature. You could substitute sweet potato or beetroot for any of the vegetables in this recipe, while the rosemary could be exchanged for thyme. I like to serve these with a simply grilled fish.

Serves 4–6

1 small butternut squash, cut into 1cm (½in) thick slices

2 large carrots, cut into quarters

2 small parsnips, cut into quarters

2 small white turnips, cut into quarters

1 red onion, cut into 6 wedges

4 garlic cloves, peeled

4 fresh rosemary sprigs

1 lemon, cut into wedges

3 tablespoons olive oil

salt and freshly ground black pepper

Step one Preheat the oven to 200°C/400°F/gas 6.

Step two Tip all the vegetables and garlic into a large roasting tin – you may need to use two. Add the rosemary sprigs and lemon wedges and then drizzle the olive oil on top, tossing to coat. Season generously and roast for 35–40 minutes or until the vegetables are just tender and lightly charred, tossing occasionally. Spoon into a serving dish and serve immediately or at room temperature.

Chocolate and Pear Upside-down Pud

This is the ultimate cheat's pud because it uses ready-made muffins, but is none the worse for that.

Step one Pre-heat the oven to 200°C/400°F/gas 6. Thickly smear the bottom of a 20cm (8in) ovenproof frying pan with the butter and sprinkle over the sugar.

Step two Peel the pears, cut them into halves or quarters and remove the cores. Put them in a bowl and toss them with the lemon juice to stop them from going brown. Drain off any excess juice, then tip them into the prepared frying pan. Place over a medium heat and cook for 7–10 minutes, shaking the pan occasionally to stop the pears from sticking, until the butter and sugar caramelize and turn toffee-coloured and the pears are just tender. You might need to lower the heat a little, depending on how quickly the pears are cooking.

Step three Crumble the chocolate muffins into small pieces and scatter them evenly over the pears. Cover with an ovenproof plate or the base of a flan tin, press down gently to bind everything together slightly, and leave the plate in place. Transfer to the oven and bake for 10 minutes, or until the pears are completely tender but still holding their shape.

Step four Remove the frying pan from the oven and leave the pudding to cool for 30 minutes so that all the juices have time to be well absorbed and the caramel can set slightly.

Step five To serve, remove the plate and loosen the edges of the pudding with a round-bladed knife. Cover the top of the pan with an inverted serving plate, take hold of both the plate and the pan, then turn them over together. Remove the frying pan, checking to see that the pudding is now on the plate, and serve cut into wedges with a spoonful of crème fraîche.

Serves 6

75g (3oz) unsalted butter, softened

75g (3oz) caster sugar

4 ripe but firm dessert pears, such as Williams

juice of 1 lemon

6 double-chocolate muffins

to serve

crème fraîche

Passion Fruit Soufflé Shells

If you're looking for a dessert that's truly stunning, look no further. These passion fruit shells really do titillate the taste buds!

Serves 4

6 large passion fruit
100ml (3½ fl oz) milk
1 egg, separated
40g (3½ oz) golden caster sugar
2 tsp plain flour
icing sugar, for dusting

Step one Preheat the oven to 200°C/400°F/gas 6. Halve the passion fruit lengthways and scoop the flesh and seeds into a small bowl. Cut a small slice off the base of the passion fruit shells and sit them snugly side by side in a heatproof dish.

Step two Gently warm the milk, but don't allow it to boil. Meanwhile, using a hand whisk, beat the egg yolk with about half the sugar until pale and light. Whisk in the flour and then the milk, over a low heat, beating until smooth. Cook gently for 2 minutes until thickened, then remove from the heat. Stir in 2 tablespoons of the passion fruit pulp and seeds.

Step three Whisk the egg white until it forms soft peaks, then add the remaining sugar and whisk until fairly stiff. Gently fold into the custard then divide between the passion fruit shells. Bake for 8 minutes until risen and golden.

Step four Meanwhile, press the remaining passion fruit pulp and seeds through a sieve into a small bowl. Discard the seeds, reserving the juice. Pour the juice into a small pan and heat gently for 2–3 minutes, stirring until slightly thickened.

Step five Place 3 soufflé shells on each serving plate. Drizzle round the passion fruit juice, dust with icing sugar and serve immediately, as they will start to sink as soon as they come out of the oven.

Chilli-glazed Mango with Yoghurt

The combination of flavours in this dessert will revive even the most jaded of palates. You'll need roughly 550g (1¼lb) of mango chunks in total.

Step one Preheat the grill. Place the yoghurt in a serving bowl and mix in the mint. Cut the mango flesh into large chunks.

Step two Melt the butter in a small pan or in the microwave. Place the mango in a large bowl and pour over the melted butter, tossing to coat evenly.

Step three Line the grill rack with foil and arrange the buttered mango on top in an even layer. Sift the icing sugar and chilli powder into a small bowl, then tip into an icing-sugar duster or sieve. Sprinkle over the mango and then cook for 8–10 minutes, turning occasionally, until the mango is heated through and has caramelized.

Step four Leave the mango pieces to 'set' for about 5 minutes, then serve with the minted yoghurt.

Serves 4

285g (9½ oz) Greek yoghurt

1 tbsp chopped fresh mint

2 large mangoes, peeled and flesh cut away from the stone

50g (2oz) butter

25g (1oz) icing sugar

¼ tsp hot chilli powder

Shrikhand with Poached Cardamom Apricots

Shrikhand is a form of strained yoghurt from the Gujarat region of India. It takes a little time to make, but if you're in a hurry, use any good-quality natural or Greek yoghurt, which is already strained, instead, and jump to step four. Clear honey may be used instead of caster sugar, if preferred.

Serves 4

2 x 500g (1lb 2oz) pots natural yoghurt

2 tbsp milk

pinch of saffron

150g (5½ oz) caster sugar, plus extra if needed

1–2 tsp rosewater, depending on strength

juice of 3 oranges

300g (11oz) ready-to-eat dried apricots

2 cardamom pods, lightly crushed

50g (2oz) shelled pistachios, roughly chopped

Step one Set a sieve over a bowl and line it with a couple of layers of clean muslin. Tip the yoghurt into the sieve and cover loosely with clingfilm. Chill for at least 3 hours, but preferably overnight, by which time the excess liquid will have drained from the yoghurt.

Step two Gently heat the milk in a small pan or in the microwave. Add the saffron and infuse for about 1 hour.

Step three Tip the yoghurt into a mixing bowl, add the saffron milk, 100g (4oz) of the sugar and the rosewater. Beat until smooth, taste and add more sugar if you like. Cover and chill until needed.

Step four Place the orange juice and apricots in a saucepan. Add the cardamom pods and the remaining sugar. Simmer gently for 5 minutes, then remove from the heat and allow to cool completely.

Step five Divide the shrikhand between four bowls, spoon the apricots and orange syrup over it, scatter with the pistachios and serve.

Orange Flower, Yoghurt and Pistachio Pudding

You just have to try this recipe for a beautiful, light pudding with a gorgeous moist base. Orange flower water is available from most large supermarkets or from specialist food stores; it has a wonderfully fragrant flavour. For an extra special touch, stir a splash of vanilla extract into some Greek yoghurt and serve with the pudding.

Serves 4

3 eggs, separated

75g (3oz) caster sugar

1 tbsp plain flour

1 tbsp orange flower water

grated zest and juice of 1 lemon

300ml (½ pint) thick Greek yoghurt

40g (1½ oz) shelled unsalted pistachios, roughly chopped

to serve

crème fraîche or vanilla ice cream

Step one Preheat the oven to 160°C/325°F/gas 3. Butter and line a 23cm (9in) spring-form cake tin. Place the egg yolks and sugar in a large bowl and, using an electric beater or wooden spoon, beat until pale and fluffy. Fold in the flour, orange flower water, lemon zest and juice until well combined. Finally stir in the yoghurt and half the pistachio nuts.

Step two Whisk the egg whites in a separate large bowl until stiff peaks form. Stir 1 spoonful of beaten egg whites into the yoghurt mixture to loosen it, then gently fold in the remaining egg white, being careful not to knock out too much air.

Step three Spoon the mixture into the prepared cake tin and bake for 20 minutes. Remove from the oven, sprinkle the remaining pistachio nuts over the top, increase the heat to 180°C/350°F/gas 4 and cook for a further 15 minutes until the pudding has risen and is golden brown.

Step four Remove the pudding from the oven and leave to cool for about 5 minutes – don't worry if it sinks slightly, as that's supposed to happen. Spoon the warm pudding onto plates, and serve with a dollop of crème fraîche or vanilla ice cream.

Hot-grilled Peaches with Pistachio Brittle

I love this dessert because of all the different textures you get in one mouthful! Sweet, sticky peaches with cool, creamy yoghurt and crisp, nutty brittle … who needs whipped cream? This pudding tastes absolutely great without it.

Serves 4

100g (4oz) caster sugar

25g (1oz) shelled pistachio nuts, roughly chopped

4 ripe peaches, halved and stoned

4 tbsp port

2 tbsp redcurrant jelly

200g (7oz) Greek yoghurt

Step one Preheat the grill to high. Line a baking tray with a silicon liner (see tip, below). Sprinkle two-thirds of the sugar into the base of a heavy-based pan, sprinkle over the pistacho nuts and heat gently until the sugar has dissolved. Increase the heat and cook for a further 2–3 minutes until the mixture is a golden colour. Immediately pour the mixture onto the lined baking tray and leave to cool and harden. (It's essential that you do this quickly as the sugar turns from golden to black in seconds.)

Step two Meanwhile, put the peaches, cut-sides up, into a heatproof dish. Warm the port and redcurrant jelly together in a small pan until runny. Pour over the peaches. Sprinkle the remaining sugar over the peaches and grill for 8–10 minutes until sticky and golden.

Step three Spoon the peaches and sauce onto serving plates, with a dollop of yoghurt at the side. Roughly break up the pistachio brittle and scatter over the top.

I always use silicon liners, which are available from most good cook shops. They are black baking liners made from silicon components. They're great as you can wash them and use them again and again.

Cheat's Banoffee Pie with Chocolate Drizzle

Traditionally this pie is made in a pastry case and calls for boiling an unopened tin of condensed milk in a deep pan of water for 5 hours. But the good news is that you can now buy banoffee toffee ready-made in jars. If you can't find it, drizzle some toffee ice-cream sauce over the bananas instead.

Step one Lightly oil a 23cm (9in) loose-bottomed flan tin that is 4cm (1½in) deep. Put the biscuits into a plastic bag and crush into fine crumbs using a rolling pin. Melt the butter in a medium-sized pan and stir in the crushed biscuits. Press the mixture onto the base and sides of the prepared flan tin. Chill for 15 minutes.

Step two Spread the banoffee toffee sauce over the base of the biscuit case and cover with the sliced bananas.

Step three In a bowl lightly whip together the cream, instant coffee and caster sugar until the mixture just forms soft peaks. Spoon this on top of the bananas and spread it out to make a seal with the edge of the biscuit case. Swirl the top attractively and chill for at least 1 hour.

Step four To serve, carefully remove the pie from the tin, drizzle with the warm melted chocolate and cut into wedges.

Serves 6

vegetable oil, for greasing

225g (8oz) digestive biscuits

100g (4oz) butter

1 x 450g (1lb) jar banoffee toffee sauce

2 large ripe bananas, peeled and sliced

450ml (¾ pint) double cream

¾ tsp instant coffee powder

1 tbsp caster sugar

to serve

25g (1oz) plain or milk chocolate, melted

Quick Blueberry, Lemon and Crème Fraîche Cheesecake

This cheesecake is extra easy because it does not require any gelatine. The action of the lemon juice on the cream cheese and crème fraîche helps it set all on its own.

Serves 8

2 large lemons

225g (8oz) full-fat cream cheese

100g (4oz) caster sugar

200g (7oz) crème fraîche

for the base

100g (4oz) butter

225g (8oz) digestive biscuits

1½ tbsp demerara sugar

for the blueberry topping

3 tbsp lemon juice

50g (2oz) caster sugar

150g (5½oz) blueberries

1 tsp arrowroot

Step one To make the base, put the butter into a large pan and melt over a low heat. Put the biscuits into a large plastic bag, seal the end and crush with a rolling pin into fine crumbs. Stir into the butter, along with the demerara sugar. Press the mixture firmly onto the base and sides of a lightly oiled 20cm (8in) loose-bottomed flan tin using the back of a spoon. Chill while you make the filling.

Step two Finely grate the zest from one lemon and squeeze the juice from both – you should get 150ml (5fl oz) of juice. In a bowl beat together the cream cheese, sugar and lemon zest until smooth. Very gradually, beat in the lemon juice until you have a thick, creamy mixture, then gently fold in the crème fraîche. Spoon the filling into the biscuit case, swirl the top with a knife and chill for at least 2 hours.

Step three To make the topping, put the lemon juice and sugar into a small pan and leave over a low heat until the sugar has dissolved. Add the blueberries, bring to a gentle simmer and cook for 1 minute. Mix the arrowroot with 1 teaspoon of cold water, stir in and cook for about 30 seconds until thickened. Transfer to a bowl and leave to cool. Then cover and chill alongside the cheesecake.

Step four Remove the cheesecake from the flan tin and transfer it to a serving plate. Spoon over the blueberry topping, cut into wedges and serve.

Clare's Chocolate, Coffee and Cardamom Mousse

My wife Clare calls this 'spread-it-on-me-thighs mousse'! It's rich, light and fluffy ... but amazingly it's low in fat! Good-quality chocolate makes all the difference, so try to get chocolate with a minimum of 50% cocoa solids. Mmm.

Step one Place 4 x 120ml (4fl oz) ramekins or serving glasses in the fridge; this will help the mousses to set quickly.

Step two Break the chocolate into chunks, then put in a large heatproof bowl with the coffee and cardamom seeds. Set over a pan of simmering water for about 3 minutes until the chocolate has melted, stirring occasionally with a wooden spoon and making sure that the bowl is not touching the hot water. Remove from the heat and set aside to cool slightly.

Step three Once the chocolate has cooled for a few minutes, beat in the egg yolks one at a time, using a wooden spoon. Place the egg whites in a separate bowl and, using a balloon whisk or an electric beater, whisk to soft peaks. Tip the sugar into the stiff whites and continue to whisk until the mixture is glossy and meringue-like.

Step four Stir a spoonful of the whites into the melted chocolate – this helps to loosen the mixture – then carefully and lightly fold in the rest of the meringue. Spoon the mixture into the chilled ramekins or glasses and chill for at least 40 minutes (or up to 2 hours if time allows). Serve on plates with a good dollop of crème fraîche topped with a little grated chocolate, if liked.

Serves 4

130g (4¾oz) plain chocolate, plus extra for grating

85ml (3fl oz) cold strong black coffee (espresso is great)

2 cardamom pods, husks discarded and seeds lightly crushed

2 eggs, separated

2 tbsp caster sugar

to serve

crème fraîche

grated chocolate (optional)

Deep Apple Soured Cream Pie

A little indulgence is a wonderful thing and it doesn't come much better than this – crisp, buttery pastry filled with creamy apples and luscious prunes, and topped with melt-in-the-mouth crumble.

Serves 4

175g (6oz) sweet shortcrust pastry

75g (3oz) plain flour, plus 1 tbsp and extra for dusting

4 Granny Smith apples

juice of 1 lemon

100g (4oz) ready-to-eat prunes, stoned and halved

2 pieces stem ginger preserved in syrup, drained and finely chopped

100g (4oz) caster sugar

1 egg

120ml (4fl oz) double cream

1 tsp ground cinnamon

50g (2oz) light muscovado sugar

50g (2oz) unsalted butter, diced and chilled, plus extra for greasing

to serve

pouring custard, cream or ice cream

Step one Preheat the oven to 200°C/400°F/gas 6. Lightly grease a 20cm (8in) loose-bottomed flan tin that is 4cm (1½in) deep. Roll out the pastry as thinly as possible on a lightly floured surface and use it to line the prepared flan tin. Prick the base here and there with a fork and chill for 20 minutes to rest the pastry and reduce shrinkage during cooking.

Step two Line the pastry case with a crumpled sheet of grease-proof paper and cover the base with a layer of baking beans. Bake for 15 minutes until the pastry case looks cooked, then remove the paper and beans and return the case to the oven for 5 minutes or so until the pastry is crisp and biscuit-coloured around the edges. Remove and reduce the oven temperature to 180°C/350°F/gas 4.

Step three Peel, core and cut the apples into wedges. Place them in a large bowl and toss in the lemon juice to prevent discoloration, then stir in the prunes and stem ginger. Whisk together the caster sugar and egg until thickened, then gently whisk in 1 tablespoon of flour and stir in the cream. Fold into the apple mixture.

Step four To make the crumble topping, sieve the remaining flour and the cinnamon into a bowl, then stir in the muscovado sugar and rub in the butter until the mixture resembles fine breadcrumbs.

Step five When the pastry case has cooled, carefully pour in the apple mixture, piling it high in the centre as the apples will shrink as they cook. Sprinkle the crumble on top in an even layer and bake for 45–50 minutes until the apple mixture is set and the crumble is lightly golden.

Jamaican Sticky Toffee Pudding

An all-time favourite in our house, this pudding also works with Madeira cake, chocolate marble cake or even banana bread.

Step one Preheat the oven to 180°C/350°F/gas 4. Cut each ginger cake into eight slices. Select an ovenproof dish that's big enough to accommodate all the slices and arrange them inside in a slightly overlapping layer.

Step two Place the butter in a pan along with the sugar and golden syrup. Bring to the boil, then reduce the heat and simmer for a minute or two, stirring occasionally, until the sugar has dissolved and a bubbling and lightly golden caramel has formed. Mix the cream into the caramel and simmer for a further few minutes, stirring occasionally, until you have a toffee sauce.

Step three Pour the toffee sauce over the cake slices and bake for 15–20 minutes until bubbling. Serve straight to the table, with more cream if you like.

Serves 4–6

2 x 275g (9½ oz) Jamaican ginger cakes

50g (2oz) butter

100g (4oz) light muscovado sugar

120ml (4fl oz) pouring golden syrup

150ml (¼ pint) double cream, plus extra for serving (optional)

Have you made this recipe? Tell us what you think at
www.mykitchentable.co.uk/blog

KITCHEN
TABLE

Chocolate Fruit and Nut Fridge Cake

As my old pastry chef Aldo would say, 'Respect the cioccolato, it's a beautiful thing'. This recipe is very versatile because you can use a mixture of whatever dried fruit and nuts you have to hand. Add a handful of mini marshmallows if you're making the cake for the children, and maybe think about using chocolate with a lower cocoa fat content. I usually add a little extra honey.

Serves 6–8

350g (12oz) plain chocolate

75g (3oz) unsalted butter

2 tbsp clear honey

1 large egg, beaten

250g (9oz) mixed dried fruit, such as glacé cherries, ready-to-eat apricots, sultanas and raisins

100g (4oz) toasted nuts, such as hazelnuts and almonds

100g (4oz) ginger biscuits

Step one Line a small roasting tin or 20cm (8in) cake tin with baking parchment or clingfilm. Break the chocolate into chunks into a heatproof bowl and melt gently, either in a microwave or over a pan of simmering water. (Don't let the bowl touch the water – just let the hot steam melt it.) When nice and smooth, mix in the butter and honey, stirring until melted and thoroughly combined. Slowly beat in the egg for a good minute, then remove from the heat.

Step two Halve the cherries and roughly chop the apricots and nuts. Tip the biscuits into a plastic bag and bash a couple of times with a rolling pin to break them into smallish pieces, not crumbs. Add the nuts, dried fruit and biscuits to the melted chocolate mixture and fold in thoroughly.

Step three Spoon into the prepared tin, level out with a spatula and leave to cool. When cold, cover lightly with clingfilm and chill until set – normally 3–4 hours.

Step four Peel off the clingfilm and cut into small squares.

I've used ginger biscuits here, but the recipe would easily work with digestives or oaty biscuits. To make it fancier, add a little chopped stem ginger or finely chopped candied peel.

10 9 8 7 6 5 4 3 2 1

Published in 2011 by BBC Books, an imprint of
Ebury Publishing, a Random House Group company

Recipes © Ainsley Harriott 2011

Book design © Woodlands Books Ltd 2011

Photography © Woodland Books Ltd 2011: pp. 6, 9, 10, 17, 25, 34,
46, 54, 61, 69, 74, 85, 113, 118, 130, 145, 150, 153, 170, 178, 185,
Gus Filgate; pp. 62, 73, 90, 98, 105, 109, 129, 137, 146, 154, 157,
158, 165, 166, 169, 182, 186, 194, 197, 201, Juliet Piddington; p. 65
William Reavell; pp. 18, 21, 30, 41, 42, 45, 50, 53, 57, 58, 66, 70, 78,
89, 94, 101, 102, 106, 110, 116, 121, 122, 125, 126, 138, 141, 149,
161, 173, 177, 181, 190, 193, 198, Howard Shooter; pp. 13, 22, 26, 29,
37, 38, 49, 81, 82, 86, 93, 97, 114, 133, 134, 162, 189, 205 Francesca
Yorke. Photography pp. 14, 33, 76, 143, 174, 202 © Dan Jones 2011;
p. 4 © Muir Vidler 2011.

All recipes contained in this book first appeared in:
Gourmet Express 1 & 2 (2000 & 2003)
Low Fat Meals in Minutes (2002)
All New Meals in Minutes (2003)
Friends and Family Cookbook (2004)
Ainsley Harriott's Ultimate Barbecue Bible (2005),
The Feel-Good Cookbook (2006)
Just Five Ingredients (2009)

Ainsley Harriott has asserted his right to be identified as the author
of this Work in accordance with the Copyright, Designs and Patents
Act 1988

The Random House Group Limited Reg. No. 954009

Addresses for companies within the Random House Group can be
found at www.randomhouse.co.uk

A CIP catalogue record for this book is available from
the British Library

ISBN: 978 1 84 990150 5

The Random House Group Limited supports The Forest
Stewardship Council (FSC), the leading international forest
certification organization. All our titles that are printed on
Greenpeace approved FSC certified paper carry the FSC logo.
Our paper procurement policy can be found at
www.rbooks.co.uk/environment

Commissioning Editor: Muna Reyal
Project Editor: Caroline McArthur
Designer: Lucy Stephens
Copy-editor: Marion Moisy
Production: Helen Everson

Colour origination by AltaImage
Printed and bound in the UK at Butler Tanner and Dennis Ltd

To buy books by your favourite authors and register
for offers visit www.rbooks.co.uk